This book belongs to

_____

_____

_____

_____

_____

PROJECT:	CREATED FOR:
DATE STARTED:	DATE COMPLETED:

CANDLE TYPE ◯ GLASSES ◯ JARS ◯ OTHER _____

WAX TYPE & BAND	QTY	MELT TEMP	POUR TEMP

ROOM TEMP:	COST:

SUPPLIES USED: _____

ADDITIVES USED: _____

INGREDIENTS	AMOUNT USED / SIZE	NOTES

AMBIENT ROOM TEMP:		NUMBER OF POURS
◯ CONTAINER	◯ MOLD	
COOLING TIME	FINAL PRODUCT	HOT THROW : 1 2 3 4 5
		COLD THROW: 1 2 3 4 5
MELT POOL:	DIFFICULTY	
	◯ EASY ◯ MODERATE ◯ CHALLENGE	

SCENT
☆☆☆☆☆

BURN LENGTH
☆☆☆☆☆

OVERALL
☆☆☆☆☆

NOTES: _____
_____
_____
_____
_____
_____

PROJECT:	CREATED FOR:
DATE STARTED:	DATE COMPLETED:

CANDLE TYPE ◯ GLASSES ◯ JARS ◯ OTHER _____

WAX TYPE & BAND	QTY	MELT TEMP	POUR TEMP

ROOM TEMP:	COST:

SUPPLIES USED: _____

ADDITIVES USED: _____

INGREDIENTS	AMOUNT USED / SIZE	NOTES

AMBIENT ROOM TEMP:		NUMBER OF POURS
◯ CONTAINER	◯ MOLD	
COOLING TIME	FINAL PRODUCT	HOT THROW : 1 2 3 4 5
		COLD THROW: 1 2 3 4 5
MELT POOL:	DIFFICULTY	
	◯ EASY ◯ MODERATE ◯ CHALLENGE	

SCENT
☆☆☆☆☆

BURN LENGTH
☆☆☆☆☆

OVERALL
☆☆☆☆☆

NOTES:
_____
_____
_____
_____
_____
_____

PROJECT:	CREATED FOR:
DATE STARTED:	DATE COMPLETED:

CANDLE TYPE ◯ GLASSES ◯ JARS ◯ OTHER _____

WAX TYPE & BAND	QTY	MELT TEMP	POUR TEMP

ROOM TEMP:	COST:

SUPPLIES USED: _____

ADDITIVES USED: _____

INGREDIENTS	AMOUNT USED / SIZE	NOTES

AMBIENT ROOM TEMP:		NUMBER OF POURS
◯ CONTAINER ◯ MOLD		
COOLING TIME	FINAL PRODUCT	HOT THROW : 1 2 3 4 5
		COLD THROW: 1 2 3 4 5
MELT POOL:	DIFFICULTY	
	◯ EASY ◯ MODERATE ◯ CHALLENGE	

SCENT
☆☆☆☆☆

BURN LENGTH
☆☆☆☆☆

OVERALL
☆☆☆☆☆

NOTES:
_____
_____
_____
_____
_____
_____

PROJECT:	CREATED FOR:
DATE STARTED:	DATE COMPLETED:

CANDLE TYPE ◯ GLASSES ◯ JARS ◯ OTHER _____

WAX TYPE & BAND	QTY	MELT TEMP	POUR TEMP

ROOM TEMP:	COST:

SUPPLIES USED: _____

ADDITIVES USED: _____

INGREDIENTS	AMOUNT USED / SIZE	NOTES

AMBIENT ROOM TEMP:		NUMBER OF POURS
◯ CONTAINER	◯ MOLD	
COOLING TIME	FINAL PRODUCT	HOT THROW : 1 2 3 4 5
		COLD THROW: 1 2 3 4 5
MELT POOL:	DIFFICULTY	
	◯ EASY ◯ MODERATE ◯ CHALLENGE	

SCENT
☆☆☆☆☆

BURN LENGTH
☆☆☆☆☆

OVERALL
☆☆☆☆☆

NOTES:
_____
_____
_____
_____
_____
_____

PROJECT:	CREATED FOR:
DATE STARTED:	DATE COMPLETED:

CANDLE TYPE ◯ GLASSES ◯ JARS ◯ OTHER _____

WAX TYPE & BAND	QTY	MELT TEMP	POUR TEMP

ROOM TEMP:	COST:

SUPPLIES USED: _____

ADDITIVES USED: _____

INGREDIENTS	AMOUNT USED / SIZE	NOTES

AMBIENT ROOM TEMP:		NUMBER OF POURS
◯ CONTAINER	◯ MOLD	
COOLING TIME	FINAL PRODUCT	HOT THROW : 1 2 3 4 5
		COLD THROW: 1 2 3 4 5
MELT POOL:	DIFFICULTY	
	◯ EASY ◯ MODERATE ◯ CHALLENGE	

SCENT
☆☆☆☆☆

BURN LENGTH
☆☆☆☆☆

OVERALL
☆☆☆☆☆

NOTES:
_____
_____
_____
_____
_____
_____

PROJECT:	CREATED FOR:
DATE STARTED:	DATE COMPLETED:

CANDLE TYPE ◯ GLASSES ◯ JARS ◯ OTHER _____

WAX TYPE & BAND	QTY	MELT TEMP	POUR TEMP

ROOM TEMP:	COST:

SUPPLIES USED: _____

ADDITIVES USED: _____

INGREDIENTS	AMOUNT USED / SIZE	NOTES

AMBIENT ROOM TEMP:		NUMBER OF POURS
◯ CONTAINER	◯ MOLD	
COOLING TIME	FINAL PRODUCT	HOT THROW : 1 2 3 4 5
		COLD THROW: 1 2 3 4 5
MELT POOL:	DIFFICULTY	
	◯ EASY ◯ MODERATE ◯ CHALLENGE	

SCENT
☆☆☆☆☆

BURN LENGTH
☆☆☆☆☆

OVERALL
☆☆☆☆☆

NOTES:
_____
_____
_____
_____
_____
_____

PROJECT: | CREATED FOR:
DATE STARTED: | DATE COMPLETED:

CANDLE TYPE ◯ GLASSES ◯ JARS ◯ OTHER _____

WAX TYPE & BAND	QTY	MELT TEMP	POUR TEMP

ROOM TEMP: | COST:

SUPPLIES USED: _____

ADDITIVES USED: _____

INGREDIENTS	AMOUNT USED / SIZE	NOTES

AMBIENT ROOM TEMP:		NUMBER OF POURS
◯ CONTAINER	◯ MOLD	
COOLING TIME	FINAL PRODUCT	HOT THROW : 1 2 3 4 5
		COLD THROW: 1 2 3 4 5
MELT POOL:	DIFFICULTY	
	◯ EASY ◯ MODERATE ◯ CHALLENGE	

SCENT
☆☆☆☆☆

BURN LENGTH
☆☆☆☆☆

OVERALL
☆☆☆☆☆

NOTES: _____
_____
_____
_____
_____
_____

PROJECT:	CREATED FOR:
DATE STARTED:	DATE COMPLETED:

CANDLE TYPE ◯ GLASSES ◯ JARS ◯ OTHER _____

WAX TYPE & BAND	QTY	MELT TEMP	POUR TEMP

ROOM TEMP:	COST:

SUPPLIES USED: _____

ADDITIVES USED: _____

INGREDIENTS	AMOUNT USED / SIZE	NOTES

AMBIENT ROOM TEMP:		NUMBER OF POURS
◯ CONTAINER	◯ MOLD	
COOLING TIME	FINAL PRODUCT	HOT THROW : 1 2 3 4 5
		COLD THROW: 1 2 3 4 5
MELT POOL:	DIFFICULTY	
	◯ EASY ◯ MODERATE ◯ CHALLENGE	

SCENT
☆☆☆☆☆

BURN LENGTH
☆☆☆☆☆

OVERALL
☆☆☆☆☆

NOTES: _____
_____
_____
_____
_____
_____

PROJECT:	CREATED FOR:
DATE STARTED:	DATE COMPLETED:

CANDLE TYPE ⭕ GLASSES ⭕ JARS ⭕ OTHER _____

WAX TYPE & BAND	QTY	MELT TEMP	POUR TEMP

ROOM TEMP:	COST:

SUPPLIES USED: _____

ADDITIVES USED: _____

INGREDIENTS	AMOUNT USED / SIZE	NOTES

AMBIENT ROOM TEMP:		NUMBER OF POURS
⭕ CONTAINER	⭕ MOLD	
COOLING TIME	FINAL PRODUCT	HOT THROW : 1 2 3 4 5
		COLD THROW: 1 2 3 4 5
MELT POOL:	DIFFICULTY	
	⭕ EASY ⭕ MODERATE ⭕ CHALLENGE	

SCENT
☆☆☆☆☆

BURN LENGTH
☆☆☆☆☆

OVERALL
☆☆☆☆☆

NOTES: _____
_____
_____
_____
_____
_____

PROJECT:	CREATED FOR:
DATE STARTED:	DATE COMPLETED:

CANDLE TYPE ○ GLASSES ○ JARS ○ OTHER _____

WAX TYPE & BAND	QTY	MELT TEMP	POUR TEMP

ROOM TEMP:	COST·

SUPPLIES USED: _____

ADDITIVES USED: _____

INGREDIENTS	AMOUNT USED / SIZE	NOTES

AMBIENT ROOM TEMP:		NUMBER OF POURS
○ CONTAINER	○ MOLD	
COOLING TIME	FINAL PRODUCT	HOT THROW : 1 2 3 4 5
		COLD THROW: 1 2 3 4 5
MELT POOL:	DIFFICULTY	
	○ EASY ○ MODERATE ○ CHALLENGE	

SCENT
☆☆☆☆☆

BURN LENGTH
☆☆☆☆☆

OVERALL
☆☆☆☆☆

NOTES:
_____
_____
_____
_____
_____
_____

PROJECT:	CREATED FOR:
DATE STARTED:	DATE COMPLETED:

CANDLE TYPE ◯ GLASSES ◯JARS ◯OTHER _____

WAX TYPE & BAND	QTY	MELT TEMP	POUR TEMP

ROOM TEMP:	COST:

SUPPLIES USED: _____

ADDITIVES USED: _____

INGREDIENTS	AMOUNT USED / SIZE	NOTES

AMBIENT ROOM TEMP:		NUMBER OF POURS
◯ CONTAINER	◯ MOLD	
COOLING TIME	FINAL PRODUCT	HOT THROW : 1 2 3 4 5
		COLD THROW: 1 2 3 4 5
MELT POOL:	DIFFICULTY	
	◯ EASY ◯MODERATE ◯CHALLENGE	

SCENT
☆☆☆☆☆

BURN LENGTH
☆☆☆☆☆

OVERALL
☆☆☆☆☆

NOTES: _____
_____
_____
_____
_____
_____

PROJECT:	CREATED FOR:
DATE STARTED:	DATE COMPLETED:

CANDLE TYPE ◯ GLASSES ◯ JARS ◯ OTHER _____

WAX TYPE & BAND	QTY	MELT TEMP	POUR TEMP

ROOM TEMP:	COST:

SUPPLIES USED: _____

ADDITIVES USED: _____

INGREDIENTS	AMOUNT USED / SIZE	NOTES

AMBIENT ROOM TEMP:	NUMBER OF POURS
◯ CONTAINER ◯ MOLD	

COOLING TIME	FINAL PRODUCT	HOT THROW : 1 2 3 4 5
		COLD THROW: 1 2 3 4 5

MELT POOL:	DIFFICULTY
	◯ EASY ◯ MODERATE ◯ CHALLENGE

SCENT
☆☆☆☆☆

BURN LENGTH
☆☆☆☆☆

OVERALL
☆☆☆☆☆

NOTES: _____
_____
_____
_____
_____
_____

PROJECT:	CREATED FOR:
DATE STARTED:	DATE COMPLETED:

CANDLE TYPE ◯ GLASSES ◯ JARS ◯ OTHER _____

WAX TYPE & BAND	QTY	MELT TEMP	POUR TEMP

ROOM TEMP:	COST:

SUPPLIES USED: _____

ADDITIVES USED: _____

INGREDIENTS	AMOUNT USED / SIZE	NOTES

AMBIENT ROOM TEMP:		NUMBER OF POURS
◯ CONTAINER	◯ MOLD	
COOLING TIME	FINAL PRODUCT	HOT THROW : 1 2 3 4 5 COLD THROW: 1 2 3 4 5
MELT POOL:	DIFFICULTY ◯ EASY ◯ MODERATE ◯ CHALLENGE	

SCENT
☆☆☆☆☆

BURN LENGTH
☆☆☆☆☆

OVERALL
☆☆☆☆☆

NOTES: _____
_____
_____
_____
_____
_____

PROJECT:	CREATED FOR:
DATE STARTED:	DATE COMPLETED:

CANDLE TYPE ◯ GLASSES ◯ JARS ◯ OTHER _____

WAX TYPE & BAND	QTY	MELT TEMP	POUR TEMP

ROOM TEMP:	COST:

SUPPLIES USED: _____

ADDITIVES USED: _____

INGREDIENTS	AMOUNT USED / SIZE	NOTES

AMBIENT ROOM TEMP:		NUMBER OF POURS
◯ CONTAINER	◯ MOLD	
COOLING TIME	FINAL PRODUCT	HOT THROW : 1 2 3 4 5
		COLD THROW: 1 2 3 4 5
MELT POOL:	DIFFICULTY	
	◯ EASY ◯ MODERATE ◯ CHALLENGE	

SCENT
☆☆☆☆☆

BURN LENGTH
☆☆☆☆☆

OVERALL
☆☆☆☆☆

NOTES: _____
_____
_____
_____
_____
_____

PROJECT:	CREATED FOR:
DATE STARTED:	DATE COMPLETED:

CANDLE TYPE ◯ GLASSES ◯ JARS ◯ OTHER _____

WAX TYPE & BAND	QTY	MELT TEMP	POUR TEMP

ROOM TEMP:	COST:

SUPPLIES USED: _____

ADDITIVES USED: _____

INGREDIENTS	AMOUNT USED / SIZE	NOTES

AMBIENT ROOM TEMP:		NUMBER OF POURS
◯ CONTAINER	◯ MOLD	
COOLING TIME	FINAL PRODUCT	HOT THROW : 1 2 3 4 5
		COLD THROW: 1 2 3 4 5
MELT POOL:	DIFFICULTY	
	◯ EASY ◯ MODERATE ◯ CHALLENGE	

SCENT
☆☆☆☆☆

BURN LENGTH
☆☆☆☆☆

OVERALL
☆☆☆☆☆

NOTES:
_____
_____
_____
_____
_____
_____

PROJECT:	CREATED FOR:
DATE STARTED:	DATE COMPLETED:

CANDLE TYPE ○ GLASSES ○JARS ○OTHER _____

WAX TYPE & BAND	QTY	MELT TEMP	POUR TEMP

ROOM TEMP:	COST:

SUPPLIES USED: _____

ADDITIVES USED: _____

INGREDIENTS	AMOUNT USED / SIZE	NOTES

AMBIENT ROOM TEMP:		NUMBER OF POURS
○ CONTAINER	○ MOLD	
COOLING TIME	FINAL PRODUCT	HOT THROW : 1 2 3 4 5
		COLD THROW: 1 2 3 4 5
MELT POOL:	DIFFICULTY	
	○ EASY ○MODERATE ○CHALLENGE	

SCENT
☆☆☆☆☆

BURN LENGTH
☆☆☆☆☆

OVERALL
☆☆☆☆☆

NOTES:
_____
_____
_____
_____
_____
_____

PROJECT:	CREATED FOR:
DATE STARTED:	DATE COMPLETED:

CANDLE TYPE ◯ GLASSES ◯JARS ◯OTHER _____

WAX TYPE & BAND	QTY	MELT TEMP	POUR TEMP

ROOM TEMP:	COST:

SUPPLIES USED: _____

ADDITIVES USED: _____

INGREDIENTS	AMOUNT USED / SIZE	NOTES

AMBIENT ROOM TEMP:		NUMBER OF POURS
◯ CONTAINER	◯ MOLD	
COOLING TIME	FINAL PRODUCT	HOT THROW : 1 2 3 4 5
		COLD THROW: 1 2 3 4 5
MELT POOL:	DIFFICULTY	
	◯ EASY ◯MODERATE ◯CHALLENGE	

SCENT
☆☆☆☆☆

BURN LENGTH
☆☆☆☆☆

OVERALL
☆☆☆☆☆

NOTES:
_____
_____
_____
_____
_____
_____

PROJECT:	CREATED FOR:
DATE STARTED:	DATE COMPLETED:

CANDLE TYPE ◯ GLASSES ◯JARS ◯OTHER _____

WAX TYPE & BAND	QTY	MELT TEMP	POUR TEMP

ROOM TEMP:	COST:

SUPPLIES USED: _____

ADDITIVES USED: _____

INGREDIENTS	AMOUNT USED / SIZE	NOTES

AMBIENT ROOM TEMP:		NUMBER OF POURS
◯ CONTAINER	◯ MOLD	
COOLING TIME	FINAL PRODUCT	HOT THROW : 1 2 3 4 5
		COLD THROW: 1 2 3 4 5
MELT POOL:	DIFFICULTY	
	◯ EASY ◯MODERATE ◯CHALLENGE	

SCENT
☆☆☆☆☆

BURN LENGTH
☆☆☆☆☆

OVERALL
☆☆☆☆☆

NOTES: _____
_____
_____
_____
_____
_____

PROJECT:	CREATED FOR:
DATE STARTED:	DATE COMPLETED:

CANDLE TYPE ◯ GLASSES ◯ JARS ◯ OTHER _____

WAX TYPE & BAND	QTY	MELT TEMP	POUR TEMP

ROOM TEMP:	COST:

SUPPLIES USED: _____

ADDITIVES USED: _____

INGREDIENTS	AMOUNT USED / SIZE	NOTES

AMBIENT ROOM TEMP:		NUMBER OF POURS
◯ CONTAINER	◯ MOLD	
COOLING TIME	FINAL PRODUCT	HOT THROW : 1 2 3 4 5
		COLD THROW: 1 2 3 4 5
MELT POOL:	DIFFICULTY	
	◯ EASY ◯ MODERATE ◯ CHALLENGE	

SCENT
☆☆☆☆☆

BURN LENGTH
☆☆☆☆☆

OVERALL
☆☆☆☆☆

NOTES:
_____
_____
_____
_____
_____
_____

PROJECT:	CREATED FOR:
DATE STARTED:	DATE COMPLETED:

CANDLE TYPE ◯ GLASSES ◯ JARS ◯ OTHER _____

WAX TYPE & BAND	QTY	MELT TEMP	POUR TEMP

ROOM TEMP.	COST:

SUPPLIES USED: _____

ADDITIVES USED: _____

INGREDIENTS	AMOUNT USED / SIZE	NOTES

AMBIENT ROOM TEMP:		NUMBER OF POURS
◯ CONTAINER	◯ MOLD	
COOLING TIME	**FINAL PRODUCT**	HOT THROW : 1 2 3 4 5
		COLD THROW: 1 2 3 4 5
MELT POOL:	**DIFFICULTY**	
	◯ EASY ◯ MODERATE ◯ CHALLENGE	

SCENT
☆☆☆☆☆

BURN LENGTH
☆☆☆☆☆

OVERALL
☆☆☆☆☆

NOTES:
_____
_____
_____
_____
_____
_____

PROJECT:	CREATED FOR:
DATE STARTED:	DATE COMPLETED:

CANDLE TYPE ◯ GLASSES ◯ JARS ◯ OTHER _____

WAX TYPE & BAND	QTY	MELT TEMP	POUR TEMP

ROOM TEMP:	COST:

SUPPLIES USED: _____

ADDITIVES USED: _____

INGREDIENTS	AMOUNT USED / SIZE	NOTES

AMBIENT ROOM TEMP:		NUMBER OF POURS
◯ CONTAINER	◯ MOLD	
COOLING TIME	FINAL PRODUCT	HOT THROW : 1 2 3 4 5
		COLD THROW: 1 2 3 4 5
MELT POOL:	DIFFICULTY	
	◯ EASY ◯ MODERATE ◯ CHALLENGE	

SCENT
☆☆☆☆☆

BURN LENGTH
☆☆☆☆☆

OVERALL
☆☆☆☆☆

NOTES:
_____
_____
_____
_____
_____
_____

PROJECT:	CREATED FOR:
DATE STARTED:	DATE COMPLETED:

CANDLE TYPE ◯ GLASSES ◯ JARS ◯ OTHER _____

WAX TYPE & BAND	QTY	MELT TEMP	POUR TEMP

ROOM TEMP:	COST:

SUPPLIES USED: _____

ADDITIVES USED: _____

INGREDIENTS	AMOUNT USED / SIZE	NOTES

AMBIENT ROOM TEMP:		NUMBER OF POURS
◯ CONTAINER	◯ MOLD	
COOLING TIME	FINAL PRODUCT	HOT THROW : 1 2 3 4 5 COLD THROW: 1 2 3 4 5
MELT POOL:	DIFFICULTY ◯ EASY ◯ MODERATE ◯ CHALLENGE	

SCENT
☆☆☆☆☆

BURN LENGTH
☆☆☆☆☆

OVERALL
☆☆☆☆☆

NOTES: _____
_____
_____
_____
_____
_____

PROJECT:	CREATED FOR:
DATE STARTED:	DATE COMPLETED:

CANDLE TYPE ◯ GLASSES ◯JARS ◯OTHER _____

WAX TYPE & BAND	QTY	MELT TEMP	POUR TEMP

ROOM TEMP:	COST:

SUPPLIES USED: _____

ADDITIVES USED: _____

INGREDIENTS	AMOUNT USED / SIZE	NOTES

AMBIENT ROOM TEMP:		NUMBER OF POURS
◯ CONTAINER	◯ MOLD	
COOLING TIME	FINAL PRODUCT	HOT THROW : 1 2 3 4 5
		COLD THROW: 1 2 3 4 5
MELT POOL:	DIFFICULTY	
	◯ EASY ◯MODERATE ◯CHALLENGE	

SCENT
☆☆☆☆☆

BURN LENGTH
☆☆☆☆☆

OVERALL
☆☆☆☆☆

NOTES: _____
_____
_____
_____
_____
_____

PROJECT:	CREATED FOR:
DATE STARTED:	DATE COMPLETED:

CANDLE TYPE ◯ GLASSES ◯ JARS ◯ OTHER _____

WAX TYPE & BAND	QTY	MELT TEMP	POUR TEMP

ROOM TEMP:	COST:

SUPPLIES USED: _____

ADDITIVES USED: _____

INGREDIENTS	AMOUNT USED / SIZE	NOTES

AMBIENT ROOM TEMP:		NUMBER OF POURS
◯ CONTAINER ◯ MOLD		
COOLING TIME	FINAL PRODUCT	HOT THROW : 1 2 3 4 5
		COLD THROW: 1 2 3 4 5
MELT POOL:	DIFFICULTY	
	◯ EASY ◯ MODERATE ◯ CHALLENGE	

SCENT
☆☆☆☆☆

BURN LENGTH
☆☆☆☆☆

OVERALL
☆☆☆☆☆

NOTES:
_____
_____
_____
_____
_____
_____

PROJECT:	CREATED FOR:
DATE STARTED:	DATE COMPLETED:

CANDLE TYPE ◯ GLASSES ◯ JARS ◯ OTHER _____

WAX TYPE & BAND	QTY	MELT TEMP	POUR TEMP

ROOM TEMP:	COST:

SUPPLIES USED: _____

ADDITIVES USED: _____

INGREDIENTS	AMOUNT USED / SIZE	NOTES

AMBIENT ROOM TEMP:		NUMBER OF POURS
◯ CONTAINER	◯ MOLD	
COOLING TIME	FINAL PRODUCT	HOT THROW : 1 2 3 4 5
		COLD THROW: 1 2 3 4 5
MELT POOL:	DIFFICULTY	
	◯ EASY ◯ MODERATE ◯ CHALLENGE	

SCENT
☆☆☆☆☆

BURN LENGTH
☆☆☆☆☆

OVERALL
☆☆☆☆☆

NOTES:
_____
_____
_____
_____
_____
_____
_____

PROJECT:	CREATED FOR:
DATE STARTED:	DATE COMPLETED:

CANDLE TYPE ◯ GLASSES ◯ JARS ◯ OTHER _____

WAX TYPE & BAND	QTY	MELT TEMP	POUR TEMP

ROOM TEMP:	COST:

SUPPLIES USED: _____

ADDITIVES USED: _____

INGREDIENTS	AMOUNT USED / SIZE	NOTES

AMBIENT ROOM TEMP:		NUMBER OF POURS
◯ CONTAINER	◯ MOLD	
COOLING TIME	FINAL PRODUCT	HOT THROW : 1 2 3 4 5 COLD THROW: 1 2 3 4 5
MELT POOL:	DIFFICULTY ◯ EASY ◯ MODERATE ◯ CHALLENGE	

SCENT
☆☆☆☆☆

BURN LENGTH
☆☆☆☆☆

OVERALL
☆☆☆☆☆

NOTES: _____
_____
_____
_____
_____
_____

PROJECT:	CREATED FOR:
DATE STARTED:	DATE COMPLETED:

CANDLE TYPE ◯ GLASSES ◯ JARS ◯ OTHER _____

WAX TYPE & BAND	QTY	MELT TEMP	POUR TEMP

ROOM TEMP:	COST:

SUPPLIES USED: _____

ADDITIVES USED: _____

INGREDIENTS	AMOUNT USED / SIZE	NOTES

AMBIENT ROOM TEMP:		NUMBER OF POURS
◯ CONTAINER ◯ MOLD		
COOLING TIME	FINAL PRODUCT	HOT THROW : 1 2 3 4 5
		COLD THROW: 1 2 3 4 5
MELT POOL:	DIFFICULTY	
	◯ EASY ◯ MODERATE ◯ CHALLENGE	

SCENT
☆☆☆☆☆

BURN LENGTH
☆☆☆☆☆

OVERALL
☆☆☆☆☆

NOTES: _____
_____
_____
_____
_____
_____

PROJECT:	CREATED FOR:
DATE STARTED:	DATE COMPLETED:

CANDLE TYPE ◯ GLASSES ◯JARS ◯OTHER _____

WAX TYPE & BAND	QTY	MELT TEMP	POUR TEMP

ROOM TEMP:	COST:

SUPPLIES USED: _____

ADDITIVES USED: _____

INGREDIENTS	AMOUNT USED / SIZE	NOTES

AMBIENT ROOM TEMP:		NUMBER OF POURS
◯ CONTAINER	◯ MOLD	
COOLING TIME	FINAL PRODUCT	HOT THROW : 1 2 3 4 5
		COLD THROW: 1 2 3 4 5
MELT POOL:	DIFFICULTY	
	◯ EASY ◯MODERATE ◯CHALLENGE	

SCENT
☆☆☆☆☆

BURN LENGTH
☆☆☆☆☆

OVERALL
☆☆☆☆☆

NOTES: _____
_____
_____
_____
_____
_____

PROJECT:	CREATED FOR:
DATE STARTED:	DATE COMPLETED:

CANDLE TYPE ◯ GLASSES ◯ JARS ◯ OTHER _____

WAX TYPE & BAND	QTY	MELT TEMP	POUR TEMP

ROOM TEMP:	COST:

SUPPLIES USED: _____

ADDITIVES USED: _____

INGREDIENTS	AMOUNT USED / SIZE	NOTES

AMBIENT ROOM TEMP:	NUMBER OF POURS
◯ CONTAINER ◯ MOLD	

COOLING TIME	FINAL PRODUCT	HOT THROW : 1 2 3 4 5
		COLD THROW: 1 2 3 4 5

MELT POOL:	DIFFICULTY
	◯ EASY ◯ MODERATE ◯ CHALLENGE

SCENT
☆☆☆☆☆

BURN LENGTH
☆☆☆☆☆

OVERALL
☆☆☆☆☆

NOTES:
_____
_____
_____
_____
_____
_____

PROJECT:	CREATED FOR:
DATE STARTED:	DATE COMPLETED:

CANDLE TYPE ◯ GLASSES ◯ JARS ◯ OTHER _____

WAX TYPE & BAND	QTY	MELT TEMP	POUR TEMP

ROOM TEMP:	COST:

SUPPLIES USED: _____

ADDITIVES USED: _____

INGREDIENTS	AMOUNT USED / SIZE	NOTES

AMBIENT ROOM TEMP:		NUMBER OF POURS
◯ CONTAINER	◯ MOLD	
COOLING TIME	FINAL PRODUCT	HOT THROW : 1 2 3 4 5
		COLD THROW: 1 2 3 4 5
MELT POOL:	DIFFICULTY	
	◯ EASY ◯ MODERATE ◯ CHALLENGE	

SCENT
☆☆☆☆☆

BURN LENGTH
☆☆☆☆☆

OVERALL
☆☆☆☆☆

NOTES:
_____
_____
_____
_____
_____
_____

PROJECT:	CREATED FOR:
DATE STARTED:	DATE COMPLETED:

CANDLE TYPE ⃝ GLASSES ⃝ JARS ⃝ OTHER _____

WAX TYPE & BAND	QTY	MELT TEMP	POUR TEMP

ROOM TEMP:	COST:

SUPPLIES USED: _____

ADDITIVES USED: _____

INGREDIENTS	AMOUNT USED / SIZE	NOTES

AMBIENT ROOM TEMP:		NUMBER OF POURS
⃝ CONTAINER	⃝ MOLD	
COOLING TIME	FINAL PRODUCT	HOT THROW : 1 2 3 4 5
		COLD THROW: 1 2 3 4 5
MELT POOL:	DIFFICULTY	
	⃝ EASY ⃝ MODERATE ⃝ CHALLENGE	

SCENT
☆☆☆☆☆

BURN LENGTH
☆☆☆☆☆

OVERALL
☆☆☆☆☆

NOTES: _____
_____
_____
_____
_____
_____

PROJECT:	CREATED FOR:
DATE STARTED:	DATE COMPLETED:

CANDLE TYPE ◯ GLASSES ◯JARS ◯OTHER _____

WAX TYPE & BAND	QTY	MELT TEMP	POUR TEMP

ROOM TEMP:	COST:

SUPPLIES USED: _____

ADDITIVES USED: _____

INGREDIENTS	AMOUNT USED / SIZE	NOTES

AMBIENT ROOM TEMP:		NUMBER OF POURS
◯ CONTAINER	◯ MOLD	
COOLING TIME	FINAL PRODUCT	HOT THROW : 1 2 3 4 5
		COLD THROW: 1 2 3 4 5
MELT POOL:	DIFFICULTY	
	◯ EASY ◯MODERATE ◯CHALLENGE	

SCENT
☆☆☆☆☆

BURN LENGTH
☆☆☆☆☆

OVERALL
☆☆☆☆☆

NOTES: _____
_____
_____
_____
_____
_____

PROJECT:	CREATED FOR:
DATE STARTED:	DATE COMPLETED:

CANDLE TYPE ◯ GLASSES ◯ JARS ◯ OTHER _____

WAX TYPE & BAND	QTY	MELT TEMP	POUR TEMP

ROOM TEMP:	COST:

SUPPLIES USED: _____

ADDITIVES USED: _____

INGREDIENTS	AMOUNT USED / SIZE	NOTES

AMBIENT ROOM TEMP:		NUMBER OF POURS
◯ CONTAINER	◯ MOLD	
COOLING TIME	FINAL PRODUCT	HOT THROW : 1 2 3 4 5
		COLD THROW: 1 2 3 4 5
MELT POOL:	DIFFICULTY	
	◯ EASY ◯ MODERATE ◯ CHALLENGE	

SCENT
☆☆☆☆☆

BURN LENGTH
☆☆☆☆☆

OVERALL
☆☆☆☆☆

NOTES: _____
_____
_____
_____
_____
_____

PROJECT:	CREATED FOR:
DATE STARTED:	DATE COMPLETED:

CANDLE TYPE ◯ GLASSES ◯JARS ◯OTHER _____

WAX TYPE & BAND	QTY	MELT TEMP	POUR TEMP

ROOM TEMP:	COST:

SUPPLIES USED: _____

ADDITIVES USED: _____

INGREDIENTS	AMOUNT USED / SIZE	NOTES

AMBIENT ROOM TEMP:		NUMBER OF POURS
◯ CONTAINER	◯ MOLD	
COOLING TIME	FINAL PRODUCT	HOT THROW : 1 2 3 4 5
		COLD THROW: 1 2 3 4 5
MELT POOL:	DIFFICULTY	
	◯ EASY ◯MODERATE ◯CHALLENGE	

SCENT
☆☆☆☆☆

BURN LENGTH
☆☆☆☆☆

OVERALL
☆☆☆☆☆

NOTES:
_____
_____
_____
_____
_____
_____

PROJECT:	CREATED FOR:
DATE STARTED:	DATE COMPLETED:

CANDLE TYPE ◯ GLASSES ◯JARS ◯OTHER _____

WAX TYPE & BAND	QTY	MELT TEMP	POUR TEMP

ROOM TEMP:	COST:

SUPPLIES USED: _____

ADDITIVES USED: _____

INGREDIENTS	AMOUNT USED / SIZE	NOTES

AMBIENT ROOM TEMP:		NUMBER OF POURS
◯ CONTAINER	◯ MOLD	
COOLING TIME	FINAL PRODUCT	HOT THROW : 1 2 3 4 5
		COLD THROW: 1 2 3 4 5
MELT POOL:	DIFFICULTY	
	◯ EASY ◯MODERATE ◯CHALLENGE	

SCENT
☆☆☆☆☆

BURN LENGTH
☆☆☆☆☆

OVERALL
☆☆☆☆☆

NOTES: _____
_____
_____
_____
_____
_____
_____

PROJECT:	CREATED FOR:
DATE STARTED:	DATE COMPLETED:

CANDLE TYPE ◯ GLASSES ◯ JARS ◯ OTHER _____

WAX TYPE & BAND	QTY	MELT TEMP	POUR TEMP

ROOM TEMP:	COST:

SUPPLIES USED: _____

ADDITIVES USED: _____

INGREDIENTS	AMOUNT USED / SIZE	NOTES

AMBIENT ROOM TEMP:		NUMBER OF POURS
◯ CONTAINER ◯ MOLD		
COOLING TIME	FINAL PRODUCT	HOT THROW : 1 2 3 4 5
		COLD THROW: 1 2 3 4 5
MELT POOL:	DIFFICULTY	
	◯ EASY ◯ MODERATE ◯ CHALLENGE	

SCENT
☆☆☆☆☆

BURN LENGTH
☆☆☆☆☆

OVERALL
☆☆☆☆☆

NOTES: _____
_____
_____
_____
_____
_____

PROJECT:	CREATED FOR:
DATE STARTED:	DATE COMPLETED:

CANDLE TYPE ◯ GLASSES ◯ JARS ◯ OTHER _____

WAX TYPE & BAND	QTY	MELT TEMP	POUR TEMP

ROOM TEMP:	COST:

SUPPLIES USED: _____

ADDITIVES USED: _____

INGREDIENTS	AMOUNT USED / SIZE	NOTES

AMBIENT ROOM TEMP:		NUMBER OF POURS
◯ CONTAINER	◯ MOLD	
COOLING TIME	FINAL PRODUCT	HOT THROW : 1 2 3 4 5
		COLD THROW: 1 2 3 4 5
MELT POOL:	DIFFICULTY	
	◯ EASY ◯ MODERATE ◯ CHALLENGE	

SCENT
☆☆☆☆☆

BURN LENGTH
☆☆☆☆☆

OVERALL
☆☆☆☆☆

NOTES:
_____
_____
_____
_____
_____
_____

PROJECT:	CREATED FOR:
DATE STARTED:	DATE COMPLETED:

CANDLE TYPE ◯ GLASSES ◯JARS ◯OTHER _____

WAX TYPE & BAND	QTY	MELT TEMP	POUR TEMP

ROOM TEMP:	COST:

SUPPLIES USED: _____

ADDITIVES USED: _____

INGREDIENTS	AMOUNT USED / SIZE	NOTES

AMBIENT ROOM TEMP:		NUMBER OF POURS
◯ CONTAINER	◯ MOLD	
COOLING TIME	FINAL PRODUCT	HOT THROW : 1 2 3 4 5
		COLD THROW: 1 2 3 4 5
MELT POOL:	DIFFICULTY	
	◯ EASY ◯MODERATE ◯CHALLENGE	

SCENT
☆☆☆☆☆

BURN LENGTH
☆☆☆☆☆

OVERALL
☆☆☆☆☆

NOTES:
_____
_____
_____
_____
_____
_____

PROJECT:	CREATED FOR:
DATE STARTED:	DATE COMPLETED:

CANDLE TYPE ○ GLASSES ○ JARS ○ OTHER _____

WAX TYPE & BAND	QTY	MELT TEMP	POUR TEMP

ROOM TEMP:	COST:

SUPPLIES USED: _____

ADDITIVES USED: _____

INGREDIENTS	AMOUNT USED / SIZE	NOTES

AMBIENT ROOM TEMP:		NUMBER OF POURS
○ CONTAINER	○ MOLD	
COOLING TIME	FINAL PRODUCT	HOT THROW : 1 2 3 4 5
		COLD THROW: 1 2 3 4 5
MELT POOL:	DIFFICULTY	
	○ EASY ○ MODERATE ○ CHALLENGE	

SCENT
☆☆☆☆☆

BURN LENGTH
☆☆☆☆☆

OVERALL
☆☆☆☆☆

NOTES: _____
_____
_____
_____
_____
_____

PROJECT:	CREATED FOR:
DATE STARTED:	DATE COMPLETED:

CANDLE TYPE ◯ GLASSES ◯JARS ◯OTHER _____

WAX TYPE & BAND	QTY	MELT TEMP	POUR TEMP

ROOM TEMP:	COST:

SUPPLIES USED: _____

ADDITIVES USED: _____

INGREDIENTS	AMOUNT USED / SIZE	NOTES

AMBIENT ROOM TEMP:		NUMBER OF POURS
◯ CONTAINER	◯ MOLD	
COOLING TIME	FINAL PRODUCT	HOT THROW : 1 2 3 4 5 COLD THROW: 1 2 3 4 5
MELT POOL:	DIFFICULTY ◯ EASY ◯MODERATE ◯CHALLENGE	

SCENT
☆☆☆☆☆

BURN LENGTH
☆☆☆☆☆

OVERALL
☆☆☆☆☆

NOTES: _____
_____
_____
_____
_____
_____

PROJECT:	CREATED FOR:
DATE STARTED:	DATE COMPLETED:

CANDLE TYPE ◯ GLASSES ◯ JARS ◯ OTHER _____

WAX TYPE & BAND	QTY	MELT TEMP	POUR TEMP

ROOM TEMP:	COST:

SUPPLIES USED: _____

ADDITIVES USED: _____

INGREDIENTS	AMOUNT USED / SIZE	NOTES

AMBIENT ROOM TEMP:		NUMBER OF POURS
◯ CONTAINER	◯ MOLD	
COOLING TIME	FINAL PRODUCT	HOT THROW : 1 2 3 4 5 COLD THROW: 1 2 3 4 5
MELT POOL:	DIFFICULTY	
	◯ EASY ◯ MODERATE ◯ CHALLENGE	

SCENT
☆☆☆☆☆

BURN LENGTH
☆☆☆☆☆

OVERALL
☆☆☆☆☆

NOTES:
_____
_____
_____
_____
_____
_____

PROJECT:	CREATED FOR:
DATE STARTED:	DATE COMPLETED:

CANDLE TYPE ◯ GLASSES ◯ JARS ◯ OTHER _____

WAX TYPE & BAND	QTY	MELT TEMP	POUR TEMP

ROOM TEMP:	COST:

SUPPLIES USED: _____

ADDITIVES USED: _____

INGREDIENTS	AMOUNT USED / SIZE	NOTES

AMBIENT ROOM TEMP:		NUMBER OF POURS
◯ CONTAINER	◯ MOLD	
COOLING TIME	FINAL PRODUCT	HOT THROW : 1 2 3 4 5
		COLD THROW: 1 2 3 4 5
MELT POOL:	DIFFICULTY	
	◯ EASY ◯ MODERATE ◯ CHALLENGE	

SCENT
☆☆☆☆☆

BURN LENGTH
☆☆☆☆☆

OVERALL
☆☆☆☆☆

NOTES:
_____
_____
_____
_____
_____
_____
_____

PROJECT:	CREATED FOR:
DATE STARTED:	DATE COMPLETED:

CANDLE TYPE ○ GLASSES ○ JARS ○ OTHER _____

WAX TYPE & BAND	QTY	MELT TEMP	POUR TEMP

ROOM TEMP:	COST:

SUPPLIES USED: _____

ADDITIVES USED: _____

INGREDIENTS	AMOUNT USED / SIZE	NOTES

AMBIENT ROOM TEMP:		NUMBER OF POURS
○ CONTAINER	○ MOLD	
COOLING TIME	FINAL PRODUCT	HOT THROW : 1 2 3 4 5
		COLD THROW: 1 2 3 4 5
MELT POOL:	DIFFICULTY	
	○ EASY ○ MODERATE ○ CHALLENGE	

SCENT
☆☆☆☆☆

BURN LENGTH
☆☆☆☆☆

OVERALL
☆☆☆☆☆

NOTES:
_____
_____
_____
_____
_____
_____

PROJECT:	CREATED FOR:
DATE STARTED:	DATE COMPLETED:

CANDLE TYPE ◯ GLASSES ◯ JARS ◯ OTHER _____

WAX TYPE & BAND	QTY	MELT TEMP	POUR TEMP

ROOM TEMP:	COST:

SUPPLIES USED: _____

ADDITIVES USED: _____

INGREDIENTS	AMOUNT USED / SIZE	NOTES

AMBIENT ROOM TEMP:	NUMBER OF POURS
◯ CONTAINER ◯ MOLD	

COOLING TIME	FINAL PRODUCT	HOT THROW : 1 2 3 4 5
		COLD THROW: 1 2 3 4 5

MELT POOL:	DIFFICULTY
	◯ EASY ◯ MODERATE ◯ CHALLENGE

SCENT
☆☆☆☆☆

BURN LENGTH
☆☆☆☆☆

OVERALL
☆☆☆☆☆

NOTES:
_____
_____
_____
_____
_____
_____
_____

PROJECT:	CREATED FOR:
DATE STARTED:	DATE COMPLETED:

CANDLE TYPE ◯ GLASSES ◯ JARS ◯ OTHER _____

WAX TYPE & BAND	QTY	MELT TEMP	POUR TEMP

ROOM TEMP:	COST:

SUPPLIES USED: _____

ADDITIVES USED: _____

INGREDIENTS	AMOUNT USED / SIZE	NOTES

AMBIENT ROOM TEMP:		NUMBER OF POURS
◯ CONTAINER	◯ MOLD	
COOLING TIME	FINAL PRODUCT	HOT THROW : 1 2 3 4 5 COLD THROW: 1 2 3 4 5
MELT POOL:	DIFFICULTY	
	◯ EASY ◯ MODERATE ◯ CHALLENGE	

SCENT
☆☆☆☆☆

BURN LENGTH
☆☆☆☆☆

OVERALL
☆☆☆☆☆

NOTES:
_____
_____
_____
_____
_____
_____

PROJECT:	CREATED FOR:
DATE STARTED:	DATE COMPLETED:

CANDLE TYPE ◯ GLASSES ◯ JARS ◯ OTHER _____

WAX TYPE & BAND	QTY	MELT TEMP	POUR TEMP

ROOM TEMP:	COST:

SUPPLIES USED: _____

ADDITIVES USED: _____

INGREDIENTS	AMOUNT USED / SIZE	NOTES

AMBIENT ROOM TEMP:	NUMBER OF POURS
◯ CONTAINER ◯ MOLD	

COOLING TIME	FINAL PRODUCT	HOT THROW : 1 2 3 4 5
		COLD THROW: 1 2 3 4 5

MELT POOL:	DIFFICULTY
	◯ EASY ◯ MODERATE ◯ CHALLENGE

SCENT
☆☆☆☆☆

BURN LENGTH
☆☆☆☆☆

OVERALL
☆☆☆☆☆

NOTES: _____
_____
_____
_____
_____
_____
_____

PROJECT:	CREATED FOR:
DATE STARTED:	DATE COMPLETED:

CANDLE TYPE ◯ GLASSES ◯ JARS ◯ OTHER _____

WAX TYPE & BAND	QTY	MELT TEMP	POUR TEMP

ROOM TEMP:	COST:

SUPPLIES USED: _____

ADDITIVES USED: _____

INGREDIENTS	AMOUNT USED / SIZE	NOTES

AMBIENT ROOM TEMP:		NUMBER OF POURS
◯ CONTAINER	◯ MOLD	
COOLING TIME	FINAL PRODUCT	HOT THROW : 1 2 3 4 5
		COLD THROW: 1 2 3 4 5
MELT POOL:	DIFFICULTY	
	◯ EASY ◯ MODERATE ◯ CHALLENGE	

SCENT
☆☆☆☆☆

BURN LENGTH
☆☆☆☆☆

OVERALL
☆☆☆☆☆

NOTES:
_____
_____
_____
_____
_____
_____

PROJECT:	CREATED FOR:
DATE STARTED:	DATE COMPLETED:

CANDLE TYPE ◯ GLASSES ◯JARS ◯OTHER _____

WAX TYPE & BAND	QTY	MELT TEMP	POUR TEMP
ROOM TEMP:		COST:	

SUPPLIES USED: _____

ADDITIVES USED: _____

INGREDIENTS	AMOUNT USED / SIZE	NOTES

AMBIENT ROOM TEMP:		NUMBER OF POURS
◯ CONTAINER	◯ MOLD	
COOLING TIME	FINAL PRODUCT	HOT THROW : 1 2 3 4 5
		COLD THROW: 1 2 3 4 5
MELT POOL:	DIFFICULTY	
	◯ EASY ◯MODERATE ◯CHALLENGE	

SCENT
☆☆☆☆☆

BURN LENGTH
☆☆☆☆☆

OVERALL
☆☆☆☆☆

NOTES:
_____
_____
_____
_____
_____
_____

PROJECT:	CREATED FOR:
DATE STARTED:	DATE COMPLETED:

CANDLE TYPE ◯ GLASSES ◯ JARS ◯ OTHER _____

WAX TYPE & BAND	QTY	MELT TEMP	POUR TEMP

ROOM TEMP:	COST:

SUPPLIES USED: _____

ADDITIVES USED: _____

INGREDIENTS	AMOUNT USED / SIZE	NOTES

AMBIENT ROOM TEMP: ◯ CONTAINER ◯ MOLD		NUMBER OF POURS
COOLING TIME	FINAL PRODUCT	HOT THROW : 1 2 3 4 5
		COLD THROW: 1 2 3 4 5
MELT POOL:	DIFFICULTY ◯ EASY ◯ MODERATE ◯ CHALLENGE	

SCENT
☆☆☆☆☆

BURN LENGTH
☆☆☆☆☆

OVERALL
☆☆☆☆☆

NOTES: _____
_____
_____
_____
_____
_____

PROJECT:	CREATED FOR:
DATE STARTED:	DATE COMPLETED:

CANDLE TYPE ◯ GLASSES ◯ JARS ◯ OTHER _____

WAX TYPE & BAND	QTY	MELT TEMP	POUR TEMP

ROOM TEMP:	COST:

SUPPLIES USED: _____

ADDITIVES USED: _____

INGREDIENTS	AMOUNT USED / SIZE	NOTES

AMBIENT ROOM TEMP:		NUMBER OF POURS
◯ CONTAINER	◯ MOLD	
COOLING TIME	FINAL PRODUCT	HOT THROW : 1 2 3 4 5
		COLD THROW: 1 2 3 4 5
MELT POOL:	DIFFICULTY	
	◯ EASY ◯ MODERATE ◯ CHALLENGE	

SCENT
☆☆☆☆☆

BURN LENGTH
☆☆☆☆☆

OVERALL
☆☆☆☆☆

NOTES: _____
_____
_____
_____
_____
_____

PROJECT:	CREATED FOR:
DATE STARTED:	DATE COMPLETED:

CANDLE TYPE ◯ GLASSES ◯ JARS ◯ OTHER _____

WAX TYPE & BAND	QTY	MELT TEMP	POUR TEMP

ROOM TEMP:	COST:

SUPPLIES USED: _____

ADDITIVES USED: _____

INGREDIENTS	AMOUNT USED / SIZE	NOTES

AMBIENT ROOM TEMP:		NUMBER OF POURS
◯ CONTAINER	◯ MOLD	
COOLING TIME	FINAL PRODUCT	HOT THROW : 1 2 3 4 5
		COLD THROW: 1 2 3 4 5
MELT POOL:	DIFFICULTY	
	◯ EASY ◯ MODERATE ◯ CHALLENGE	

SCENT
☆☆☆☆☆

BURN LENGTH
☆☆☆☆☆

OVERALL
☆☆☆☆☆

NOTES: _____
_____
_____
_____
_____
_____

PROJECT:	CREATED FOR:
DATE STARTED:	DATE COMPLETED:

CANDLE TYPE ◯ GLASSES ◯ JARS ◯ OTHER _____

WAX TYPE & BAND	QTY	MELT TEMP	POUR TEMP

ROOM TEMP:	COST:

SUPPLIES USED: _____

ADDITIVES USED: _____

INGREDIENTS	AMOUNT USED / SIZE	NOTES

AMBIENT ROOM TEMP:		NUMBER OF POURS
◯ CONTAINER	◯ MOLD	
COOLING TIME	FINAL PRODUCT	HOT THROW : 1 2 3 4 5
		COLD THROW: 1 2 3 4 5
MELT POOL:	DIFFICULTY	
	◯ EASY ◯ MODERATE ◯ CHALLENGE	

SCENT
☆☆☆☆☆

BURN LENGTH
☆☆☆☆☆

OVERALL
☆☆☆☆☆

NOTES:
_____
_____
_____
_____
_____

PROJECT:	CREATED FOR:
DATE STARTED:	DATE COMPLETED:

CANDLE TYPE ◯ GLASSES ◯ JARS ◯ OTHER _____

WAX TYPE & BAND	QTY	MELT TEMP	POUR TEMP

ROOM TEMP:	COST:

SUPPLIES USED: _____

ADDITIVES USED: _____

INGREDIENTS	AMOUNT USED / SIZE	NOTES

AMBIENT ROOM TEMP:		NUMBER OF POURS
◯ CONTAINER	◯ MOLD	
COOLING TIME	FINAL PRODUCT	HOT THROW : 1 2 3 4 5
		COLD THROW: 1 2 3 4 5
MELT POOL:	DIFFICULTY	
	◯ EASY ◯ MODERATE ◯ CHALLENGE	

SCENT
☆☆☆☆☆

BURN LENGTH
☆☆☆☆☆

OVERALL
☆☆☆☆☆

NOTES:
_____
_____
_____
_____
_____
_____

PROJECT:	CREATED FOR:
DATE STARTED:	DATE COMPLETED:

CANDLE TYPE ◯ GLASSES ◯JARS ◯OTHER _____

WAX TYPE & BAND	QTY	MELT TEMP	POUR TEMP
ROOM TEMP:	COST:		

SUPPLIES USED: _____

ADDITIVES USED: _____

INGREDIENTS	AMOUNT USED / SIZE	NOTES

AMBIENT ROOM TEMP:		NUMBER OF POURS
◯ CONTAINER	◯ MOLD	
COOLING TIME	FINAL PRODUCT	HOT THROW : 1 2 3 4 5 COLD THROW: 1 2 3 4 5
MELT POOL:	DIFFICULTY ◯ EASY ◯MODERATE ◯CHALLENGE	

SCENT
☆☆☆☆☆

BURN LENGTH
☆☆☆☆☆

OVERALL
☆☆☆☆☆

NOTES:
_____
_____
_____
_____
_____
_____

PROJECT:	CREATED FOR:
DATE STARTED:	DATE COMPLETED:

CANDLE TYPE ◯ GLASSES ◯JARS ◯OTHER _____

WAX TYPE & BAND	QTY	MELT TEMP	POUR TEMP

ROOM TEMP:	COST:

SUPPLIES USED: _____

ADDITIVES USED: _____

INGREDIENTS	AMOUNT USED / SIZE	NOTES

AMBIENT ROOM TEMP:		NUMBER OF POURS
◯ CONTAINER	◯ MOLD	
COOLING TIME	FINAL PRODUCT	HOT THROW : 1 2 3 4 5 COLD THROW: 1 2 3 4 5
MELT POOL:	DIFFICULTY ◯ EASY ◯MODERATE ◯CHALLENGE	

SCENT
☆☆☆☆☆

BURN LENGTH
☆☆☆☆☆

OVERALL
☆☆☆☆☆

NOTES: _____
_____
_____
_____
_____

PROJECT:	CREATED FOR:
DATE STARTED:	DATE COMPLETED:

CANDLE TYPE ◯ GLASSES ◯ JARS ◯ OTHER _____

WAX TYPE & BAND	QTY	MELT TEMP	POUR TEMP

ROOM TEMP:	COST:

SUPPLIES USED: _____

ADDITIVES USED: _____

INGREDIENTS	AMOUNT USED / SIZE	NOTES

AMBIENT ROOM TEMP:	NUMBER OF POURS
◯ CONTAINER ◯ MOLD	

COOLING TIME	FINAL PRODUCT	HOT THROW : 1 2 3 4 5
		COLD THROW: 1 2 3 4 5

MELT POOL:	DIFFICULTY
	◯ EASY ◯ MODERATE ◯ CHALLENGE

SCENT
☆☆☆☆☆

BURN LENGTH
☆☆☆☆☆

OVERALL
☆☆☆☆☆

NOTES: _____
_____
_____
_____
_____
_____

PROJECT:	CREATED FOR:
DATE STARTED:	DATE COMPLETED:

CANDLE TYPE ◯ GLASSES ◯ JARS ◯ OTHER _____

WAX TYPE & BAND	QTY	MELT TEMP	POUR TEMP

ROOM TEMP:	COST:

SUPPLIES USED: _____

ADDITIVES USED: _____

INGREDIENTS	AMOUNT USED / SIZE	NOTES

AMBIENT ROOM TEMP:		NUMBER OF POURS
◯ CONTAINER	◯ MOLD	
COOLING TIME	FINAL PRODUCT	HOT THROW : 1 2 3 4 5
		COLD THROW: 1 2 3 4 5
MELT POOL:	DIFFICULTY	
	◯ EASY ◯ MODERATE ◯ CHALLENGE	

SCENT
☆☆☆☆☆

BURN LENGTH
☆☆☆☆☆

OVERALL
☆☆☆☆☆

NOTES:
_____
_____
_____
_____
_____
_____

PROJECT:	CREATED FOR:
DATE STARTED:	DATE COMPLETED:

CANDLE TYPE ◯ GLASSES ◯ JARS ◯ OTHER _____

WAX TYPE & BAND	QTY	MELT TEMP	POUR TEMP

ROOM TEMP:	COST:

SUPPLIES USED: _____

ADDITIVES USED: _____

INGREDIENTS	AMOUNT USED / SIZE	NOTES

AMBIENT ROOM TEMP:		NUMBER OF POURS
◯ CONTAINER	◯ MOLD	
COOLING TIME	FINAL PRODUCT	HOT THROW : 1 2 3 4 5 COLD THROW: 1 2 3 4 5
MELT POOL:	DIFFICULTY ◯ EASY ◯ MODERATE ◯ CHALLENGE	

SCENT
☆☆☆☆☆

BURN LENGTH
☆☆☆☆☆

OVERALL
☆☆☆☆☆

NOTES: _____
_____
_____
_____
_____
_____

PROJECT:	CREATED FOR:
DATE STARTED:	DATE COMPLETED:

CANDLE TYPE ◯ GLASSES ◯ JARS ◯ OTHER _____

WAX TYPE & BAND	QTY	MELT TEMP	POUR TEMP

ROOM TEMP:	COST:

SUPPLIES USED: _____

ADDITIVES USED: _____

INGREDIENTS	AMOUNT USED / SIZE	NOTES

AMBIENT ROOM TEMP:		NUMBER OF POURS
◯ CONTAINER ◯ MOLD		
COOLING TIME	FINAL PRODUCT	HOT THROW : 1 2 3 4 5
		COLD THROW: 1 2 3 4 5
MELT POOL:	DIFFICULTY	
	◯ EASY ◯ MODERATE ◯ CHALLENGE	

SCENT
☆☆☆☆☆

BURN LENGTH
☆☆☆☆☆

OVERALL
☆☆☆☆☆

NOTES:
_____
_____
_____
_____
_____
_____

PROJECT:	CREATED FOR:
DATE STARTED:	DATE COMPLETED:

CANDLE TYPE ◯ GLASSES ◯ JARS ◯ OTHER _____

WAX TYPE & BAND	QTY	MELT TEMP	POUR TEMP

ROOM TEMP:	COST:

SUPPLIES USED: _____

ADDITIVES USED: _____

INGREDIENTS	AMOUNT USED / SIZE	NOTES

AMBIENT ROOM TEMP:		NUMBER OF POURS
◯ CONTAINER	◯ MOLD	
COOLING TIME	FINAL PRODUCT	HOT THROW : 1 2 3 4 5
		COLD THROW: 1 2 3 4 5
MELT POOL:	DIFFICULTY	
	◯ EASY ◯ MODERATE ◯ CHALLENGE	

SCENT
☆☆☆☆☆

BURN LENGTH
☆☆☆☆☆

OVERALL
☆☆☆☆☆

NOTES: _____
_____
_____
_____
_____

PROJECT:	CREATED FOR:
DATE STARTED:	DATE COMPLETED:

CANDLE TYPE ◯ GLASSES ◯JARS ◯OTHER _____

WAX TYPE & BAND	QTY	MELT TEMP	POUR TEMP

ROOM TEMP:	COST:

SUPPLIES USED: _____

ADDITIVES USED: _____

INGREDIENTS	AMOUNT USED / SIZE	NOTES

AMBIENT ROOM TEMP:		NUMBER OF POURS
◯ CONTAINER	◯ MOLD	
COOLING TIME	FINAL PRODUCT	HOT THROW : 1 2 3 4 5
		COLD THROW: 1 2 3 4 5
MELT POOL:	DIFFICULTY	
	◯ EASY ◯MODERATE ◯CHALLENGE	

SCENT
☆☆☆☆☆

BURN LENGTH
☆☆☆☆☆

OVERALL
☆☆☆☆☆

NOTES: _____
_____
_____
_____
_____
_____
_____

PROJECT:	CREATED FOR:
DATE STARTED:	DATE COMPLETED:

CANDLE TYPE ◯ GLASSES ◯ JARS ◯ OTHER _____

WAX TYPE & BAND	QTY	MELT TEMP	POUR TEMP

ROOM TEMP:	COST:

SUPPLIES USED: _____

ADDITIVES USED: _____

INGREDIENTS	AMOUNT USED / SIZE	NOTES

AMBIENT ROOM TEMP:		NUMBER OF POURS
◯ CONTAINER	◯ MOLD	
COOLING TIME	FINAL PRODUCT	HOT THROW : 1 2 3 4 5
		COLD THROW: 1 2 3 4 5
MELT POOL:	DIFFICULTY	
	◯ EASY ◯ MODERATE ◯ CHALLENGE	

SCENT
☆☆☆☆☆

BURN LENGTH
☆☆☆☆☆

OVERALL
☆☆☆☆☆

NOTES:
_____
_____
_____
_____
_____
_____

PROJECT:	CREATED FOR:
DATE STARTED:	DATE COMPLETED:

CANDLE TYPE ◯ GLASSES ◯ JARS ◯ OTHER _____

WAX TYPE & BAND	QTY	MELT TEMP	POUR TEMP

ROOM TEMP:	COST:

SUPPLIES USED: _____

ADDITIVES USED: _____

INGREDIENTS	AMOUNT USED / SIZE	NOTES

AMBIENT ROOM TEMP:		NUMBER OF POURS
◯ CONTAINER	◯ MOLD	
COOLING TIME	FINAL PRODUCT	HOT THROW : 1 2 3 4 5
		COLD THROW: 1 2 3 4 5
MELT POOL:	DIFFICULTY	
	◯ EASY ◯ MODERATE ◯ CHALLENGE	

SCENT
☆☆☆☆☆

BURN LENGTH
☆☆☆☆☆

OVERALL
☆☆☆☆☆

NOTES: _____
_____
_____
_____
_____
_____

PROJECT:	CREATED FOR:
DATE STARTED:	DATE COMPLETED:

CANDLE TYPE ◯ GLASSES ◯ JARS ◯ OTHER _____

WAX TYPE & BAND	QTY	MELT TEMP	POUR TEMP

ROOM TEMP:	COST:

SUPPLIES USED: _____

ADDITIVES USED: _____

INGREDIENTS	AMOUNT USED / SIZE	NOTES

AMBIENT ROOM TEMP:		NUMBER OF POURS
◯ CONTAINER	◯ MOLD	
COOLING TIME	FINAL PRODUCT	HOT THROW : 1 2 3 4 5
		COLD THROW: 1 2 3 4 5
MELT POOL:	DIFFICULTY	
	◯ EASY ◯ MODERATE ◯ CHALLENGE	

SCENT
☆☆☆☆☆

BURN LENGTH
☆☆☆☆☆

OVERALL
☆☆☆☆☆

NOTES: _____
_____
_____
_____
_____
_____

PROJECT:	CREATED FOR:
DATE STARTED:	DATE COMPLETED:

CANDLE TYPE ◯ GLASSES ◯ JARS ◯ OTHER _____

WAX TYPE & BAND	QTY	MELT TEMP	POUR TEMP

ROOM TEMP:	COST:

SUPPLIES USED: _____

ADDITIVES USED: _____

INGREDIENTS	AMOUNT USED / SIZE	NOTES

AMBIENT ROOM TEMP:		NUMBER OF POURS
◯ CONTAINER	◯ MOLD	
COOLING TIME	FINAL PRODUCT	HOT THROW : 1 2 3 4 5
		COLD THROW: 1 2 3 4 5
MELT POOL:	DIFFICULTY	
	◯ EASY ◯ MODERATE ◯ CHALLENGE	

SCENT
☆☆☆☆☆

BURN LENGTH
☆☆☆☆☆

OVERALL
☆☆☆☆☆

NOTES:
_____
_____
_____
_____
_____
_____

PROJECT:	CREATED FOR:
DATE STARTED:	DATE COMPLETED:

CANDLE TYPE ○ GLASSES ○ JARS ○ OTHER _____

WAX TYPE & BAND	QTY	MELT TEMP	POUR TEMP

ROOM TEMP:	COST:

SUPPLIES USED: _____

ADDITIVES USED: _____

INGREDIENTS	AMOUNT USED / SIZE	NOTES

AMBIENT ROOM TEMP:		NUMBER OF POURS
○ CONTAINER	○ MOLD	
COOLING TIME	FINAL PRODUCT	HOT THROW : 1 2 3 4 5
		COLD THROW: 1 2 3 4 5
MELT POOL:	DIFFICULTY	
	○ EASY ○ MODERATE ○ CHALLENGE	

SCENT
☆☆☆☆☆

BURN LENGTH
☆☆☆☆☆

OVERALL
☆☆☆☆☆

NOTES:
_____
_____
_____
_____
_____
_____

PROJECT:	CREATED FOR:
DATE STARTED:	DATE COMPLETED:

CANDLE TYPE ◯ GLASSES ◯ JARS ◯ OTHER _____

WAX TYPE & BAND	QTY	MELT TEMP	POUR TEMP

ROOM TEMP:	COST:

SUPPLIES USED: _____

ADDITIVES USED: _____

INGREDIENTS	AMOUNT USED / SIZE	NOTES

AMBIENT ROOM TEMP:		NUMBER OF POURS
◯ CONTAINER	◯ MOLD	
COOLING TIME	FINAL PRODUCT	HOT THROW : 1 2 3 4 5 COLD THROW: 1 2 3 4 5
MELT POOL:	DIFFICULTY ◯ EASY ◯ MODERATE ◯ CHALLENGE	

SCENT
☆☆☆☆☆

BURN LENGTH
☆☆☆☆☆

OVERALL
☆☆☆☆☆

NOTES:
_____
_____
_____
_____
_____
_____

PROJECT:	CREATED FOR:
DATE STARTED:	DATE COMPLETED:

CANDLE TYPE ◯ GLASSES ◯ JARS ◯ OTHER _____

WAX TYPE & BAND	QTY	MELT TEMP	POUR TEMP

ROOM TEMP:	COST:

SUPPLIES USED: _____

ADDITIVES USED: _____

INGREDIENTS	AMOUNT USED / SIZE	NOTES

AMBIENT ROOM TEMP:		NUMBER OF POURS
◯ CONTAINER	◯ MOLD	
COOLING TIME	FINAL PRODUCT	HOT THROW : 1 2 3 4 5
		COLD THROW: 1 2 3 4 5
MELT POOL:	DIFFICULTY	
	◯ EASY ◯ MODERATE ◯ CHALLENGE	

SCENT
☆☆☆☆☆

BURN LENGTH
☆☆☆☆☆

OVERALL
☆☆☆☆☆

NOTES:
_____
_____
_____
_____
_____
_____

PROJECT:	CREATED FOR:
DATE STARTED:	DATE COMPLETED:

CANDLE TYPE ◯ GLASSES ◯ JARS ◯ OTHER _____

WAX TYPE & BAND	QTY	MELT TEMP	POUR TEMP

ROOM TEMP:	COST:

SUPPLIES USED: _____

ADDITIVES USED: _____

INGREDIENTS	AMOUNT USED / SIZE	NOTES

AMBIENT ROOM TEMP:	NUMBER OF POURS
◯ CONTAINER ◯ MOLD	

COOLING TIME	FINAL PRODUCT	HOT THROW : 1 2 3 4 5
		COLD THROW: 1 2 3 4 5

MELT POOL:	DIFFICULTY
	◯ EASY ◯ MODERATE ◯ CHALLENGE

SCENT
☆☆☆☆☆

BURN LENGTH
☆☆☆☆☆

OVERALL
☆☆☆☆☆

NOTES: _____
_____
_____
_____
_____
_____

PROJECT:	CREATED FOR:
DATE STARTED:	DATE COMPLETED:

CANDLE TYPE ◯ GLASSES ◯ JARS ◯ OTHER _____

WAX TYPE & BAND	QTY	MELT TEMP	POUR TEMP

ROOM TEMP:	COST:

SUPPLIES USED: _____

ADDITIVES USED: _____

INGREDIENTS	AMOUNT USED / SIZE	NOTES

AMBIENT ROOM TEMP:		NUMBER OF POURS
◯ CONTAINER	◯ MOLD	
COOLING TIME	FINAL PRODUCT	HOT THROW : 1 2 3 4 5
		COLD THROW: 1 2 3 4 5
MELT POOL:	DIFFICULTY	
	◯ EASY ◯ MODERATE ◯ CHALLENGE	

SCENT
☆☆☆☆☆

BURN LENGTH
☆☆☆☆☆

OVERALL
☆☆☆☆☆

NOTES: _____
_____
_____
_____
_____
_____

PROJECT:	CREATED FOR:
DATE STARTED:	DATE COMPLETED:

CANDLE TYPE ◯ GLASSES ◯ JARS ◯ OTHER _____

WAX TYPE & BAND	QTY	MELT TEMP	POUR TEMP

ROOM TEMP:	COST:

SUPPLIES USED: _____

ADDITIVES USED: _____

INGREDIENTS	AMOUNT USED / SIZE	NOTES

AMBIENT ROOM TEMP:		NUMBER OF POURS
◯ CONTAINER	◯ MOLD	
COOLING TIME	FINAL PRODUCT	HOT THROW : 1 2 3 4 5
		COLD THROW: 1 2 3 4 5
MELT POOL:	DIFFICULTY	
	◯ EASY ◯ MODERATE ◯ CHALLENGE	

SCENT
☆☆☆☆☆

BURN LENGTH
☆☆☆☆☆

OVERALL
☆☆☆☆☆

NOTES: _____
_____
_____
_____
_____
_____

PROJECT:	CREATED FOR:
DATE STARTED:	DATE COMPLETED:

CANDLE TYPE ◯ GLASSES ◯ JARS ◯ OTHER _____

WAX TYPE & BAND	QTY	MELT TEMP	POUR TEMP

ROOM TEMP:	COST:

SUPPLIES USED: _____

ADDITIVES USED: _____

INGREDIENTS	AMOUNT USED / SIZE	NOTES

AMBIENT ROOM TEMP:	NUMBER OF POURS
◯ CONTAINER ◯ MOLD	

COOLING TIME	FINAL PRODUCT	HOT THROW : 1 2 3 4 5
		COLD THROW: 1 2 3 4 5

MELT POOL:	DIFFICULTY
	◯ EASY ◯ MODERATE ◯ CHALLENGE

SCENT
☆☆☆☆☆

BURN LENGTH
☆☆☆☆☆

OVERALL
☆☆☆☆☆

NOTES: _____
_____
_____
_____
_____
_____

PROJECT:	CREATED FOR:
DATE STARTED:	DATE COMPLETED:

CANDLE TYPE ◯ GLASSES ◯ JARS ◯ OTHER _____

WAX TYPE & BAND	QTY	MELT TEMP	POUR TEMP

ROOM TEMP:	COST:

SUPPLIES USED: _____

ADDITIVES USED: _____

INGREDIENTS	AMOUNT USED / SIZE	NOTES

AMBIENT ROOM TEMP:	NUMBER OF POURS
◯ CONTAINER ◯ MOLD	

COOLING TIME	FINAL PRODUCT	HOT THROW : 1 2 3 4 5
		COLD THROW: 1 2 3 4 5

MELT POOL:	DIFFICULTY
	◯ EASY ◯ MODERATE ◯ CHALLENGE

SCENT
☆☆☆☆☆

BURN LENGTH
☆☆☆☆☆

OVERALL
☆☆☆☆☆

NOTES: _____
_____
_____
_____
_____
_____
_____

PROJECT:	CREATED FOR:
DATE STARTED:	DATE COMPLETED:

CANDLE TYPE ◯ GLASSES ◯ JARS ◯ OTHER _____

WAX TYPE & BAND	QTY	MELT TEMP	POUR TEMP

ROOM TEMP:	COST:

SUPPLIES USED: _____

ADDITIVES USED: _____

INGREDIENTS	AMOUNT USED / SIZE	NOTES

AMBIENT ROOM TEMP:		NUMBER OF POURS
◯ CONTAINER ◯ MOLD		
COOLING TIME	FINAL PRODUCT	HOT THROW : 1 2 3 4 5
		COLD THROW: 1 2 3 4 5
MELT POOL:	DIFFICULTY	
	◯ EASY ◯ MODERATE ◯ CHALLENGE	

SCENT
☆☆☆☆☆

BURN LENGTH
☆☆☆☆☆

OVERALL
☆☆☆☆☆

NOTES: _____
_____
_____
_____
_____
_____
_____

PROJECT:	CREATED FOR:
DATE STARTED:	DATE COMPLETED:

CANDLE TYPE ◯ GLASSES ◯ JARS ◯ OTHER _____

WAX TYPE & BAND	QTY	MELT TEMP	POUR TEMP

ROOM TEMP:	COST:

SUPPLIES USED: _____

ADDITIVES USED: _____

INGREDIENTS	AMOUNT USED / SIZE	NOTES

AMBIENT ROOM TEMP:	NUMBER OF POURS
◯ CONTAINER ◯ MOLD	

COOLING TIME	FINAL PRODUCT	HOT THROW : 1 2 3 4 5
		COLD THROW: 1 2 3 4 5

MELT POOL:	DIFFICULTY
	◯ EASY ◯ MODERATE ◯ CHALLENGE

SCENT
☆☆☆☆☆

BURN LENGTH
☆☆☆☆☆

OVERALL
☆☆☆☆☆

NOTES:
_____
_____
_____
_____
_____
_____

PROJECT:	CREATED FOR:
DATE STARTED:	DATE COMPLETED:

CANDLE TYPE ◯ GLASSES ◯ JARS ◯ OTHER _____

WAX TYPE & BAND	QTY	MELT TEMP	POUR TEMP

ROOM TEMP:	COST:

SUPPLIES USED: _____

ADDITIVES USED: _____

INGREDIENTS	AMOUNT USED / SIZE	NOTES

AMBIENT ROOM TEMP:		NUMBER OF POURS
◯ CONTAINER	◯ MOLD	
COOLING TIME	FINAL PRODUCT	HOT THROW : 1 2 3 4 5
		COLD THROW: 1 2 3 4 5
MELT POOL:	DIFFICULTY	
	◯ EASY ◯ MODERATE ◯ CHALLENGE	

SCENT
☆☆☆☆☆

BURN LENGTH
☆☆☆☆☆

OVERALL
☆☆☆☆☆

NOTES: _____
_____
_____
_____
_____
_____

PROJECT:	CREATED FOR:
DATE STARTED:	DATE COMPLETED:

CANDLE TYPE ○ GLASSES ○ JARS ○ OTHER _____

WAX TYPE & BAND	QTY	MELT TEMP	POUR TEMP

ROOM TEMP:	COST:

SUPPLIES USED: _____

ADDITIVES USED: _____

INGREDIENTS	AMOUNT USED / SIZE	NOTES

AMBIENT ROOM TEMP:		NUMBER OF POURS
○ CONTAINER	○ MOLD	
COOLING TIME	FINAL PRODUCT	HOT THROW : 1 2 3 4 5
		COLD THROW: 1 2 3 4 5
MELT POOL:	DIFFICULTY	
	○ EASY ○ MODERATE ○ CHALLENGE	

SCENT
☆☆☆☆☆

BURN LENGTH
☆☆☆☆☆

OVERALL
☆☆☆☆☆

NOTES: _____
_____
_____
_____
_____
_____

PROJECT:	CREATED FOR:
DATE STARTED:	DATE COMPLETED:

CANDLE TYPE ◯ GLASSES ◯JARS ◯OTHER _____

WAX TYPE & BAND	QTY	MELT TEMP	POUR TEMP

ROOM TEMP:	COST:

SUPPLIES USED: _____

ADDITIVES USED: _____

INGREDIENTS	AMOUNT USED / SIZE	NOTES

AMBIENT ROOM TEMP:		NUMBER OF POURS
◯ CONTAINER	◯ MOLD	
COOLING TIME	FINAL PRODUCT	HOT THROW : 1 2 3 4 5
		COLD THROW: 1 2 3 4 5
MELT POOL:	DIFFICULTY	
	◯ EASY ◯MODERATE ◯CHALLENGE	

SCENT
☆☆☆☆☆

BURN LENGTH
☆☆☆☆☆

OVERALL
☆☆☆☆☆

NOTES:
_____
_____
_____
_____
_____
_____

PROJECT:	CREATED FOR:
DATE STARTED:	DATE COMPLETED:

CANDLE TYPE ○ GLASSES ○ JARS ○ OTHER _____

WAX TYPE & BAND	QTY	MELT TEMP	POUR TEMP

ROOM TEMP:	COST:

SUPPLIES USED: _____

ADDITIVES USED: _____

INGREDIENTS	AMOUNT USED / SIZE	NOTES

AMBIENT ROOM TEMP:		NUMBER OF POURS
○ CONTAINER	○ MOLD	
COOLING TIME	FINAL PRODUCT	HOT THROW : 1 2 3 4 5
		COLD THROW: 1 2 3 4 5
MELT POOL:	DIFFICULTY	
	○ EASY ○ MODERATE ○ CHALLENGE	

SCENT
☆☆☆☆☆

BURN LENGTH
☆☆☆☆☆

OVERALL
☆☆☆☆☆

NOTES:
_____
_____
_____
_____
_____
_____

PROJECT:	CREATED FOR:
DATE STARTED:	DATE COMPLETED:

CANDLE TYPE ◯ GLASSES ◯ JARS ◯ OTHER _____

WAX TYPE & BAND	QTY	MELT TEMP	POUR TEMP

ROOM TEMP:	COST:

SUPPLIES USED: _____

ADDITIVES USED: _____

INGREDIENTS	AMOUNT USED / SIZE	NOTES

AMBIENT ROOM TEMP:		NUMBER OF POURS
◯ CONTAINER ◯ MOLD		
COOLING TIME	FINAL PRODUCT	HOT THROW : 1 2 3 4 5
		COLD THROW: 1 2 3 4 5
MELT POOL:	DIFFICULTY	
	◯ EASY ◯ MODERATE ◯ CHALLENGE	

SCENT
☆☆☆☆☆

BURN LENGTH
☆☆☆☆☆

OVERALL
☆☆☆☆☆

NOTES: _____
_____
_____
_____
_____
_____

PROJECT:	CREATED FOR:
DATE STARTED:	DATE COMPLETED:

CANDLE TYPE ◯ GLASSES ◯JARS ◯OTHER _____

WAX TYPE & BAND	QTY	MELT TEMP	POUR TEMP

ROOM TEMP:	COST:

SUPPLIES USED: _____

ADDITIVES USED: _____

INGREDIENTS	AMOUNT USED / SIZE	NOTES

AMBIENT ROOM TEMP:		NUMBER OF POURS
◯ CONTAINER	◯ MOLD	
COOLING TIME	FINAL PRODUCT	HOT THROW : 1 2 3 4 5
		COLD THROW: 1 2 3 4 5
MELT POOL:	DIFFICULTY	
	◯ EASY ◯MODERATE ◯CHALLENGE	

SCENT
☆☆☆☆☆

BURN LENGTH
☆☆☆☆☆

OVERALL
☆☆☆☆☆

NOTES: _____
_____
_____
_____
_____
_____

PROJECT:	CREATED FOR:
DATE STARTED:	DATE COMPLETED:

CANDLE TYPE ◯ GLASSES ◯ JARS ◯ OTHER _____

WAX TYPE & BAND	QTY	MELT TEMP	POUR TEMP

ROOM TEMP:	COST:

SUPPLIES USED: _____

ADDITIVES USED: _____

INGREDIENTS	AMOUNT USED / SIZE	NOTES

AMBIENT ROOM TEMP:		NUMBER OF POURS
◯ CONTAINER	◯ MOLD	
COOLING TIME	FINAL PRODUCT	HOT THROW : 1 2 3 4 5
		COLD THROW: 1 2 3 4 5
MELT POOL:	DIFFICULTY	
	◯ EASY ◯ MODERATE ◯ CHALLENGE	

SCENT
☆☆☆☆☆

BURN LENGTH
☆☆☆☆☆

OVERALL
☆☆☆☆☆

NOTES:
_____
_____
_____
_____
_____
_____

PROJECT:	CREATED FOR:
DATE STARTED:	DATE COMPLETED:

CANDLE TYPE ◯ GLASSES ◯JARS ◯OTHER _____

WAX TYPE & BAND	QTY	MELT TEMP	POUR TEMP

ROOM TEMP:	COST:

SUPPLIES USED: _____

ADDITIVES USED: _____

INGREDIENTS	AMOUNT USED / SIZE	NOTES

AMBIENT ROOM TEMP:		NUMBER OF POURS
◯ CONTAINER	◯ MOLD	
COOLING TIME	FINAL PRODUCT	HOT THROW : 1 2 3 4 5
		COLD THROW: 1 2 3 4 5
MELT POOL:	DIFFICULTY	
	◯ EASY ◯MODERATE ◯CHALLENGE	

SCENT
☆☆☆☆☆

BURN LENGTH
☆☆☆☆☆

OVERALL
☆☆☆☆☆

NOTES: _____
_____
_____
_____
_____
_____
_____

PROJECT:	CREATED FOR:
DATE STARTED:	DATE COMPLETED:

CANDLE TYPE ◯ GLASSES ◯ JARS ◯ OTHER _____

WAX TYPE & BAND	QTY	MELT TEMP	POUR TEMP

ROOM TEMP:	COST:

SUPPLIES USED: _____

ADDITIVES USED: _____

INGREDIENTS	AMOUNT USED / SIZE	NOTES

AMBIENT ROOM TEMP:		NUMBER OF POURS
◯ CONTAINER	◯ MOLD	
COOLING TIME	FINAL PRODUCT	HOT THROW : 1 2 3 4 5 COLD THROW: 1 2 3 4 5
MELT POOL:	DIFFICULTY ◯ EASY ◯ MODERATE ◯ CHALLENGE	

SCENT
☆☆☆☆☆

BURN LENGTH
☆☆☆☆☆

OVERALL
☆☆☆☆☆

NOTES: _____
_____
_____
_____
_____
_____

PROJECT:	CREATED FOR:
DATE STARTED:	DATE COMPLETED:

CANDLE TYPE ⭘ GLASSES ⭘ JARS ⭘ OTHER _____

WAX TYPE & BAND	QTY	MELT TEMP	POUR TEMP

ROOM TEMP:	COST:

SUPPLIES USED: _____

ADDITIVES USED: _____

INGREDIENTS	AMOUNT USED / SIZE	NOTES

AMBIENT ROOM TEMP:		NUMBER OF POURS
⭘ CONTAINER	⭘ MOLD	
COOLING TIME	FINAL PRODUCT	HOT THROW : 1 2 3 4 5
		COLD THROW: 1 2 3 4 5
MELT POOL:	DIFFICULTY	
	⭘ EASY ⭘ MODERATE ⭘ CHALLENGE	

SCENT
☆☆☆☆☆

BURN LENGTH
☆☆☆☆☆

OVERALL
☆☆☆☆☆

NOTES:
_____
_____
_____
_____
_____
_____
_____

PROJECT:	CREATED FOR:
DATE STARTED:	DATE COMPLETED:

CANDLE TYPE ◯ GLASSES ◯ JARS ◯ OTHER _____

WAX TYPE & BAND	QTY	MELT TEMP	POUR TEMP

ROOM TEMP:	COST:

SUPPLIES USED: _____

ADDITIVES USED: _____

INGREDIENTS	AMOUNT USED / SIZE	NOTES

AMBIENT ROOM TEMP:		NUMBER OF POURS
◯ CONTAINER	◯ MOLD	
COOLING TIME	FINAL PRODUCT	HOT THROW : 1 2 3 4 5
		COLD THROW: 1 2 3 4 5
MELT POOL:	DIFFICULTY	
	◯ EASY ◯ MODERATE ◯ CHALLENGE	

SCENT
☆☆☆☆☆

BURN LENGTH
☆☆☆☆☆

OVERALL
☆☆☆☆☆

NOTES: _____
_____
_____
_____
_____
_____
_____

PROJECT:	CREATED FOR:
DATE STARTED:	DATE COMPLETED:

CANDLE TYPE ◯ GLASSES ◯ JARS ◯ OTHER _____

WAX TYPE & BAND	QTY	MELT TEMP	POUR TEMP

ROOM TEMP:	COST:

SUPPLIES USED: _____

ADDITIVES USED: _____

INGREDIENTS	AMOUNT USED / SIZE	NOTES

AMBIENT ROOM TEMP:		NUMBER OF POURS
◯ CONTAINER	◯ MOLD	
COOLING TIME	FINAL PRODUCT	HOT THROW : 1 2 3 4 5
		COLD THROW: 1 2 3 4 5
MELT POOL:	DIFFICULTY	
	◯ EASY ◯ MODERATE ◯ CHALLENGE	

SCENT
☆☆☆☆☆

BURN LENGTH
☆☆☆☆☆

OVERALL
☆☆☆☆☆

NOTES:
_____
_____
_____
_____
_____
_____

PROJECT:	CREATED FOR:
DATE STARTED:	DATE COMPLETED:

CANDLE TYPE ◯ GLASSES ◯ JARS ◯ OTHER _____

WAX TYPE & BAND	QTY	MELT TEMP	POUR TEMP

ROOM TEMP:	COST:

SUPPLIES USED: _____

ADDITIVES USED: _____

INGREDIENTS	AMOUNT USED / SIZE	NOTES

AMBIENT ROOM TEMP:		NUMBER OF POURS
◯ CONTAINER	◯ MOLD	
COOLING TIME	FINAL PRODUCT	HOT THROW : 1 2 3 4 5
		COLD THROW: 1 2 3 4 5
MELT POOL:	DIFFICULTY	
	◯ EASY ◯ MODERATE ◯ CHALLENGE	

SCENT
☆☆☆☆☆

BURN LENGTH
☆☆☆☆☆

OVERALL
☆☆☆☆☆

NOTES: _____
_____
_____
_____
_____
_____

PROJECT:	CREATED FOR:
DATE STARTED:	DATE COMPLETED:

CANDLE TYPE ○ GLASSES ○ JARS ○ OTHER _____

WAX TYPE & BAND	QTY	MELT TEMP	POUR TEMP

ROOM TEMP:	COST:

SUPPLIES USED: _____

ADDITIVES USED: _____

INGREDIENTS	AMOUNT USED / SIZE	NOTES

AMBIENT ROOM TEMP:		NUMBER OF POURS
○ CONTAINER	○ MOLD	
COOLING TIME	FINAL PRODUCT	HOT THROW : 1 2 3 4 5
		COLD THROW: 1 2 3 4 5
MELT POOL:	DIFFICULTY	
	○ EASY ○ MODERATE ○ CHALLENGE	

SCENT
☆☆☆☆☆

BURN LENGTH
☆☆☆☆☆

OVERALL
☆☆☆☆☆

NOTES:
_____
_____
_____
_____
_____
_____

PROJECT:	CREATED FOR:
DATE STARTED:	DATE COMPLETED:

CANDLE TYPE ◯ GLASSES ◯JARS ◯OTHER _____

WAX TYPE & BAND	QTY	MELT TEMP	POUR TEMP

ROOM TEMP:	COST:

SUPPLIES USED: _____

ADDITIVES USED: _____

INGREDIENTS	AMOUNT USED / SIZE	NOTES

AMBIENT ROOM TEMP:		NUMBER OF POURS
◯ CONTAINER	◯ MOLD	
COOLING TIME	FINAL PRODUCT	HOT THROW : 1 2 3 4 5
		COLD THROW: 1 2 3 4 5
MELT POOL:	DIFFICULTY	
	◯ EASY ◯MODERATE ◯CHALLENGE	

SCENT
☆☆☆☆☆

BURN LENGTH
☆☆☆☆☆

OVERALL
☆☆☆☆☆

NOTES:
_____
_____
_____
_____
_____
_____
_____

PROJECT:	CREATED FOR:
DATE STARTED:	DATE COMPLETED:

CANDLE TYPE ◯ GLASSES ◯ JARS ◯ OTHER _____

WAX TYPE & BAND	QTY	MELT TEMP	POUR TEMP

ROOM TEMP:	COST:

SUPPLIES USED: _____

ADDITIVES USED: _____

INGREDIENTS	AMOUNT USED / SIZE	NOTES

AMBIENT ROOM TEMP:		NUMBER OF POURS
◯ CONTAINER	◯ MOLD	
COOLING TIME	FINAL PRODUCT	HOT THROW : 1 2 3 4 5
		COLD THROW: 1 2 3 4 5
MELT POOL:	DIFFICULTY	
	◯ EASY ◯ MODERATE ◯ CHALLENGE	

SCENT
☆☆☆☆☆

BURN LENGTH
☆☆☆☆☆

OVERALL
☆☆☆☆☆

NOTES:
_____
_____
_____
_____
_____
_____

PROJECT:	CREATED FOR:
DATE STARTED:	DATE COMPLETED:

CANDLE TYPE ◯ GLASSES ◯ JARS ◯ OTHER _____

WAX TYPE & BAND	QTY	MELT TEMP	POUR TEMP

ROOM TEMP:	COST:

SUPPLIES USED: _____

ADDITIVES USED: _____

INGREDIENTS	AMOUNT USED / SIZE	NOTES

AMBIENT ROOM TEMP:		NUMBER OF POURS
◯ CONTAINER	◯ MOLD	
COOLING TIME	FINAL PRODUCT	HOT THROW : 1 2 3 4 5
		COLD THROW: 1 2 3 4 5
MELT POOL:	DIFFICULTY	
	◯ EASY ◯ MODERATE ◯ CHALLENGE	

SCENT
☆☆☆☆☆

BURN LENGTH
☆☆☆☆☆

OVERALL
☆☆☆☆☆

NOTES: _____
_____
_____
_____
_____
_____

PROJECT:	CREATED FOR:
DATE STARTED:	DATE COMPLETED:

CANDLE TYPE ◯ GLASSES ◯ JARS ◯ OTHER _____

WAX TYPE & BAND	QTY	MELT TEMP	POUR TEMP

ROOM TEMP:	COST:

SUPPLIES USED: _____

ADDITIVES USED: _____

INGREDIENTS	AMOUNT USED / SIZE	NOTES

AMBIENT ROOM TEMP:		NUMBER OF POURS
◯ CONTAINER	◯ MOLD	
COOLING TIME	FINAL PRODUCT	HOT THROW : 1 2 3 4 5
		COLD THROW: 1 2 3 4 5
MELT POOL:	DIFFICULTY	
	◯ EASY ◯ MODERATE ◯ CHALLENGE	

SCENT
☆☆☆☆☆

BURN LENGTH
☆☆☆☆☆

OVERALL
☆☆☆☆☆

NOTES: _____
_____
_____
_____
_____
_____

PROJECT:	CREATED FOR:
DATE STARTED:	DATE COMPLETED:

CANDLE TYPE ◯ GLASSES ◯JARS ◯OTHER _____

WAX TYPE & BAND	QTY	MELT TEMP	POUR TEMP

ROOM TEMP:	COST:

SUPPLIES USED: _____

ADDITIVES USED: _____

INGREDIENTS	AMOUNT USED / SIZE	NOTES

AMBIENT ROOM TEMP:		NUMBER OF POURS
◯ CONTAINER	◯ MOLD	
COOLING TIME	FINAL PRODUCT — HOT THROW : 1 2 3 4 5 / COLD THROW: 1 2 3 4 5	
MELT POOL:	DIFFICULTY / ◯EASY ◯MODERATE ◯CHALLENGE	

SCENT
☆☆☆☆☆

BURN LENGTH
☆☆☆☆☆

OVERALL
☆☆☆☆☆

NOTES:
_____
_____
_____
_____
_____
_____

PROJECT:	CREATED FOR:
DATE STARTED:	DATE COMPLETED:

CANDLE TYPE ◯ GLASSES ◯ JARS ◯ OTHER _____

WAX TYPE & BAND	QTY	MELT TEMP	POUR TEMP

ROOM TEMP:	COST:

SUPPLIES USED: _____

ADDITIVES USED: _____

INGREDIENTS	AMOUNT USED / SIZE	NOTES

AMBIENT ROOM TEMP:		NUMBER OF POURS
◯ CONTAINER	◯ MOLD	
COOLING TIME	FINAL PRODUCT	HOT THROW : 1 2 3 4 5
		COLD THROW: 1 2 3 4 5
MELT POOL:	DIFFICULTY	
	◯ EASY ◯ MODERATE ◯ CHALLENGE	

SCENT
☆☆☆☆☆

BURN LENGTH
☆☆☆☆☆

OVERALL
☆☆☆☆☆

NOTES: _____
_____
_____
_____
_____
_____

PROJECT:	CREATED FOR:
DATE STARTED:	DATE COMPLETED:

CANDLE TYPE ◯ GLASSES ◯ JARS ◯ OTHER _____

WAX TYPE & BAND	QTY	MELT TEMP	POUR TEMP

ROOM TEMP:	COST:

SUPPLIES USED: _____

ADDITIVES USED: _____

INGREDIENTS	AMOUNT USED / SIZE	NOTES

AMBIENT ROOM TEMP:		NUMBER OF POURS
◯ CONTAINER	◯ MOLD	
COOLING TIME	FINAL PRODUCT	HOT THROW : 1 2 3 4 5
		COLD THROW: 1 2 3 4 5
MELT POOL:	DIFFICULTY	
	◯ EASY ◯ MODERATE ◯ CHALLENGE	

SCENT
☆☆☆☆☆

BURN LENGTH
☆☆☆☆☆

OVERALL
☆☆☆☆☆

NOTES: _____
_____
_____
_____
_____
_____

PROJECT:	CREATED FOR:
DATE STARTED:	DATE COMPLETED:

CANDLE TYPE ◯ GLASSES ◯JARS ◯OTHER _____

WAX TYPE & BAND	QTY	MELT TEMP	POUR TEMP

ROOM TEMP:	COST:

SUPPLIES USED: _____

ADDITIVES USED: _____

INGREDIENTS	AMOUNT USED / SIZE	NOTES

AMBIENT ROOM TEMP:	NUMBER OF POURS
◯ CONTAINER ◯ MOLD	

COOLING TIME	FINAL PRODUCT	HOT THROW : 1 2 3 4 5
		COLD THROW: 1 2 3 4 5

MELT POOL:	DIFFICULTY
	◯ EASY ◯MODERATE ◯CHALLENGE

SCENT
☆☆☆☆☆

BURN LENGTH
☆☆☆☆☆

OVERALL
☆☆☆☆☆

NOTES: _____
_____
_____
_____
_____
_____

PROJECT:	CREATED FOR:
DATE STARTED:	DATE COMPLETED:

CANDLE TYPE ◯ GLASSES ◯JARS ◯OTHER _____

WAX TYPE & BAND	QTY	MELT TEMP	POUR TEMP

ROOM TEMP:	COST:

SUPPLIES USED: _____

ADDITIVES USED: _____

INGREDIENTS	AMOUNT USED / SIZE	NOTES

AMBIENT ROOM TEMP:		NUMBER OF POURS
◯ CONTAINER	◯ MOLD	
COOLING TIME	FINAL PRODUCT	HOT THROW : 1 2 3 4 5
		COLD THROW: 1 2 3 4 5
MELT POOL:	DIFFICULTY	
	◯ EASY ◯MODERATE ◯CHALLENGE	

SCENT
☆☆☆☆☆

BURN LENGTH
☆☆☆☆☆

OVERALL
☆☆☆☆☆

NOTES: _____
_____
_____
_____
_____
_____
_____

PROJECT:	CREATED FOR:
DATE STARTED:	DATE COMPLETED:

CANDLE TYPE ◯ GLASSES ◯ JARS ◯ OTHER _____

WAX TYPE & BAND	QTY	MELT TEMP	POUR TEMP

ROOM TEMP:	COST:

SUPPLIES USED: _____

ADDITIVES USED: _____

INGREDIENTS	AMOUNT USED / SIZE	NOTES

AMBIENT ROOM TEMP:		NUMBER OF POURS
◯ CONTAINER	◯ MOLD	
COOLING TIME	FINAL PRODUCT	HOT THROW : 1 2 3 4 5
		COLD THROW: 1 2 3 4 5
MELT POOL:	DIFFICULTY	
	◯ EASY ◯ MODERATE ◯ CHALLENGE	

SCENT
☆☆☆☆☆

BURN LENGTH
☆☆☆☆☆

OVERALL
☆☆☆☆☆

NOTES: _____
_____
_____
_____
_____
_____

PROJECT:	CREATED FOR:
DATE STARTED:	DATE COMPLETED:

CANDLE TYPE ◯ GLASSES ◯ JARS ◯ OTHER _____

WAX TYPE & BAND	QTY	MELT TEMP	POUR TEMP

ROOM TEMP:	COST:

SUPPLIES USED: _____

ADDITIVES USED: _____

INGREDIENTS	AMOUNT USED / SIZE	NOTES

AMBIENT ROOM TEMP:		NUMBER OF POURS
◯ CONTAINER	◯ MOLD	
COOLING TIME	FINAL PRODUCT	HOT THROW : 1 2 3 4 5
		COLD THROW: 1 2 3 4 5
MELT POOL:	DIFFICULTY	
	◯ EASY ◯ MODERATE ◯ CHALLENGE	

SCENT
☆☆☆☆☆

BURN LENGTH
☆☆☆☆☆

OVERALL
☆☆☆☆☆

NOTES: _____
_____
_____
_____
_____
_____

PROJECT:	CREATED FOR:
DATE STARTED:	DATE COMPLETED:

CANDLE TYPE ◯ GLASSES ◯ JARS ◯ OTHER _____

WAX TYPE & BAND	QTY	MELT TEMP	POUR TEMP

ROOM TEMP:	COST:

SUPPLIES USED: _____

ADDITIVES USED: _____

INGREDIENTS	AMOUNT USED / SIZE	NOTES

AMBIENT ROOM TEMP:		NUMBER OF POURS
◯ CONTAINER	◯ MOLD	
COOLING TIME	FINAL PRODUCT	HOT THROW : 1 2 3 4 5 COLD THROW: 1 2 3 4 5
MELT POOL:	DIFFICULTY	
	◯ EASY ◯ MODERATE ◯ CHALLENGE	

SCENT
☆☆☆☆☆

BURN LENGTH
☆☆☆☆☆

OVERALL
☆☆☆☆☆

NOTES:
_____
_____
_____
_____
_____
_____

PROJECT:	CREATED FOR:
DATE STARTED:	DATE COMPLETED:

CANDLE TYPE ◯ GLASSES ◯JARS ◯OTHER _____

WAX TYPE & BAND	QTY	MELT TEMP	POUR TEMP

ROOM TEMP:	COST:

SUPPLIES USED: _____

ADDITIVES USED: _____

INGREDIENTS	AMOUNT USED / SIZE	NOTES

AMBIENT ROOM TEMP:		NUMBER OF POURS
◯ CONTAINER	◯ MOLD	
COOLING TIME	FINAL PRODUCT	HOT THROW : 1 2 3 4 5
		COLD THROW: 1 2 3 4 5
MELT POOL:	DIFFICULTY	
	◯ EASY ◯MODERATE ◯CHALLENGE	

SCENT
☆☆☆☆☆

BURN LENGTH
☆☆☆☆☆

OVERALL
☆☆☆☆☆

NOTES:
_____
_____
_____
_____
_____
_____
_____

PROJECT:	CREATED FOR:
DATE STARTED:	DATE COMPLETED:

CANDLE TYPE ◯ GLASSES ◯ JARS ◯ OTHER _____

WAX TYPE & BAND	QTY	MELT TEMP	POUR TEMP
ROOM TEMP:		COST:	

SUPPLIES USED: _____

ADDITIVES USED: _____

INGREDIENTS	AMOUNT USED / SIZE	NOTES

AMBIENT ROOM TEMP:		NUMBER OF POURS
◯ CONTAINER	◯ MOLD	
COOLING TIME	FINAL PRODUCT	HOT THROW : 1 2 3 4 5
		COLD THROW: 1 2 3 4 5
MELT POOL:	DIFFICULTY	
	◯ EASY ◯ MODERATE ◯ CHALLENGE	

SCENT
☆☆☆☆☆

BURN LENGTH
☆☆☆☆☆

OVERALL
☆☆☆☆☆

NOTES:
_____
_____
_____
_____
_____
_____

PROJECT:	CREATED FOR:
DATE STARTED:	DATE COMPLETED:

CANDLE TYPE ◯ GLASSES ◯ JARS ◯ OTHER _____

WAX TYPE & BAND	QTY	MELT TEMP	POUR TEMP

ROOM TEMP:	COST:

SUPPLIES USED: _____

ADDITIVES USED: _____

INGREDIENTS	AMOUNT USED / SIZE	NOTES

AMBIENT ROOM TEMP:		NUMBER OF POURS
◯ CONTAINER	◯ MOLD	
COOLING TIME	FINAL PRODUCT	HOT THROW : 1 2 3 4 5
		COLD THROW: 1 2 3 4 5
MELT POOL:	DIFFICULTY	
	◯ EASY ◯ MODERATE ◯ CHALLENGE	

SCENT
☆☆☆☆☆

BURN LENGTH
☆☆☆☆☆

OVERALL
☆☆☆☆☆

NOTES: _____
_____
_____
_____
_____
_____

PROJECT:	CREATED FOR:
DATE STARTED:	DATE COMPLETED:

CANDLE TYPE ◯ GLASSES ◯JARS ◯OTHER _____

WAX TYPE & BAND	QTY	MELT TEMP	POUR TEMP

ROOM TEMP:	COST:

SUPPLIES USED: _____

ADDITIVES USED: _____

INGREDIENTS	AMOUNT USED / SIZE	NOTES

AMBIENT ROOM TEMP:		NUMBER OF POURS
◯ CONTAINER	◯ MOLD	
COOLING TIME	FINAL PRODUCT	HOT THROW : 1 2 3 4 5
		COLD THROW: 1 2 3 4 5
MELT POOL:	DIFFICULTY	
	◯ EASY ◯MODERATE ◯CHALLENGE	

SCENT
☆☆☆☆☆

BURN LENGTH
☆☆☆☆☆

OVERALL
☆☆☆☆☆

NOTES: _____
_____
_____
_____
_____
_____

PROJECT:	CREATED FOR:
DATE STARTED:	DATE COMPLETED:

CANDLE TYPE ◯ GLASSES ◯ JARS ◯ OTHER _____

WAX TYPE & BAND	QTY	MELT TEMP	POUR TEMP

ROOM TEMP:	COST:

SUPPLIES USED: _____

ADDITIVES USED: _____

INGREDIENTS	AMOUNT USED / SIZE	NOTES

AMBIENT ROOM TEMP:	NUMBER OF POURS
◯ CONTAINER ◯ MOLD	

COOLING TIME	FINAL PRODUCT	HOT THROW : 1 2 3 4 5
		COLD THROW: 1 2 3 4 5

MELT POOL:	DIFFICULTY
	◯ EASY ◯ MODERATE ◯ CHALLENGE

SCENT
☆☆☆☆☆

BURN LENGTH
☆☆☆☆☆

OVERALL
☆☆☆☆☆

NOTES: _____
_____
_____
_____
_____
_____

PROJECT:	CREATED FOR:
DATE STARTED:	DATE COMPLETED:

CANDLE TYPE ◯ GLASSES ◯ JARS ◯ OTHER _____

WAX TYPE & BAND	QTY	MELT TEMP	POUR TEMP

ROOM TEMP:	COST:

SUPPLIES USED: _____

ADDITIVES USED: _____

INGREDIENTS	AMOUNT USED / SIZE	NOTES

AMBIENT ROOM TEMP:		NUMBER OF POURS
◯ CONTAINER	◯ MOLD	
COOLING TIME	FINAL PRODUCT	HOT THROW : 1 2 3 4 5
		COLD THROW: 1 2 3 4 5
MELT POOL:	DIFFICULTY	
	◯ EASY ◯ MODERATE ◯ CHALLENGE	

SCENT
☆☆☆☆☆

BURN LENGTH
☆☆☆☆☆

OVERALL
☆☆☆☆☆

NOTES:
_____
_____
_____
_____
_____
_____

PROJECT:	CREATED FOR:
DATE STARTED:	DATE COMPLETED:

CANDLE TYPE ◯ GLASSES ◯JARS ◯OTHER _____

WAX TYPE & BAND	QTY	MELT TEMP	POUR TEMP

ROOM TEMP:	COST:

SUPPLIES USED: _____

ADDITIVES USED: _____

INGREDIENTS	AMOUNT USED / SIZE	NOTES

AMBIENT ROOM TEMP:		NUMBER OF POURS
◯ CONTAINER ◯ MOLD		
COOLING TIME	FINAL PRODUCT	HOT THROW : 1 2 3 4 5
		COLD THROW: 1 2 3 4 5
MELT POOL:	DIFFICULTY	
	◯ EASY ◯MODERATE ◯CHALLENGE	

SCENT
☆☆☆☆☆

BURN LENGTH
☆☆☆☆☆

OVERALL
☆☆☆☆☆

NOTES: _____
_____
_____
_____
_____
_____

PROJECT:	CREATED FOR:
DATE STARTED:	DATE COMPLETED:

CANDLE TYPE ◯ GLASSES ◯ JARS ◯ OTHER _____

WAX TYPE & BAND	QTY	MELT TEMP	POUR TEMP

ROOM TEMP:	COST:

SUPPLIES USED: _____

ADDITIVES USED: _____

INGREDIENTS	AMOUNT USED / SIZE	NOTES

AMBIENT ROOM TEMP:		NUMBER OF POURS
◯ CONTAINER	◯ MOLD	
COOLING TIME	FINAL PRODUCT	HOT THROW : 1 2 3 4 5 COLD THROW: 1 2 3 4 5
MELT POOL:	DIFFICULTY ◯ EASY ◯ MODERATE ◯ CHALLENGE	

SCENT
☆☆☆☆☆

BURN LENGTH
☆☆☆☆☆

OVERALL
☆☆☆☆☆

NOTES: _____
_____
_____
_____
_____
_____

PROJECT:	CREATED FOR:
DATE STARTED:	DATE COMPLETED:

CANDLE TYPE ◯ GLASSES ◯ JARS ◯ OTHER _____

WAX TYPE & BAND	QTY	MELT TEMP	POUR TEMP

ROOM TEMP:	COST:

SUPPLIES USED: _____

ADDITIVES USED: _____

INGREDIENTS	AMOUNT USED / SIZE	NOTES

AMBIENT ROOM TEMP:		NUMBER OF POURS
◯ CONTAINER	◯ MOLD	
COOLING TIME	FINAL PRODUCT	HOT THROW : 1 2 3 4 5
		COLD THROW: 1 2 3 4 5
MELT POOL:	DIFFICULTY	
	◯ EASY ◯ MODERATE ◯ CHALLENGE	

SCENT
☆☆☆☆☆

BURN LENGTH
☆☆☆☆☆

OVERALL
☆☆☆☆☆

NOTES: _____
_____
_____
_____
_____
_____

PROJECT:	CREATED FOR:
DATE STARTED:	DATE COMPLETED:

CANDLE TYPE ◯ GLASSES ◯ JARS ◯ OTHER _____

WAX TYPE & BAND	QTY	MELT TEMP	POUR TEMP

ROOM TEMP:	COST:

SUPPLIES USED: _____

ADDITIVES USED: _____

INGREDIENTS	AMOUNT USED / SIZE	NOTES

AMBIENT ROOM TEMP:		NUMBER OF POURS
◯ CONTAINER	◯ MOLD	
COOLING TIME	FINAL PRODUCT	HOT THROW : 1 2 3 4 5
		COLD THROW: 1 2 3 4 5
MELT POOL:	DIFFICULTY	
	◯ EASY ◯ MODERATE ◯ CHALLENGE	

SCENT
☆☆☆☆☆

BURN LENGTH
☆☆☆☆☆

OVERALL
☆☆☆☆☆

NOTES: _____
_____
_____
_____
_____
_____

PROJECT:	CREATED FOR:
DATE STARTED:	DATE COMPLETED:

CANDLE TYPE ◯ GLASSES ◯JARS ◯OTHER _____

WAX TYPE & BAND	QTY	MELT TEMP	POUR TEMP

ROOM TEMP:	COST:

SUPPLIES USED: _____

ADDITIVES USED: _____

INGREDIENTS	AMOUNT USED / SIZE	NOTES

AMBIENT ROOM TEMP:		NUMBER OF POURS
◯ CONTAINER	◯ MOLD	
COOLING TIME	FINAL PRODUCT	HOT THROW : 1 2 3 4 5
		COLD THROW: 1 2 3 4 5
MELT POOL:	DIFFICULTY	
	◯ EASY ◯MODERATE ◯CHALLENGE	

SCENT
☆☆☆☆☆

BURN LENGTH
☆☆☆☆☆

OVERALL
☆☆☆☆☆

NOTES: _____
_____
_____
_____
_____
_____

PROJECT:	CREATED FOR:
DATE STARTED:	DATE COMPLETED:

CANDLE TYPE ◯ GLASSES ◯ JARS ◯ OTHER _____

WAX TYPE & BAND	QTY	MELT TEMP	POUR TEMP

ROOM TEMP:	COST:

SUPPLIES USED: _____

ADDITIVES USED: _____

INGREDIENTS	AMOUNT USED / SIZE	NOTES

AMBIENT ROOM TEMP:		NUMBER OF POURS
◯ CONTAINER	◯ MOLD	
COOLING TIME	FINAL PRODUCT	HOT THROW : 1 2 3 4 5
		COLD THROW: 1 2 3 4 5
MELT POOL:	DIFFICULTY	
	◯ EASY ◯ MODERATE ◯ CHALLENGE	

SCENT
☆☆☆☆☆

BURN LENGTH
☆☆☆☆☆

OVERALL
☆☆☆☆☆

NOTES: _____
_____
_____
_____
_____

PROJECT:	CREATED FOR:
DATE STARTED:	DATE COMPLETED:

CANDLE TYPE ◯ GLASSES ◯JARS ◯OTHER _____

WAX TYPE & BAND	QTY	MELT TEMP	POUR TEMP

ROOM TEMP:	COST.

SUPPLIES USED: _____

ADDITIVES USED: _____

INGREDIENTS	AMOUNT USED / SIZE	NOTES

AMBIENT ROOM TEMP:		NUMBER OF POURS
◯ CONTAINER	◯ MOLD	
COOLING TIME	FINAL PRODUCT	HOT THROW : 1 2 3 4 5
		COLD THROW: 1 2 3 4 5
MELT POOL:	DIFFICULTY	
	◯ EASY ◯MODERATE ◯CHALLENGE	

SCENT
☆☆☆☆☆

BURN LENGTH
☆☆☆☆☆

OVERALL
☆☆☆☆☆

NOTES: _____
_____
_____
_____
_____
_____

PROJECT:	CREATED FOR:
DATE STARTED:	DATE COMPLETED:

CANDLE TYPE ◯ GLASSES ◯ JARS ◯ OTHER _____

WAX TYPE & BAND	QTY	MELT TEMP	POUR TEMP

ROOM TEMP:	COST:

SUPPLIES USED: _____

ADDITIVES USED: _____

INGREDIENTS	AMOUNT USED / SIZE	NOTES

AMBIENT ROOM TEMP:		NUMBER OF POURS
◯ CONTAINER	◯ MOLD	
COOLING TIME	FINAL PRODUCT	HOT THROW : 1 2 3 4 5
		COLD THROW: 1 2 3 4 5
MELT POOL:	DIFFICULTY	
	◯ EASY ◯ MODERATE ◯ CHALLENGE	

SCENT
☆☆☆☆☆

BURN LENGTH
☆☆☆☆☆

OVERALL
☆☆☆☆☆

NOTES: _____
_____
_____
_____
_____
_____

PROJECT:	CREATED FOR:
DATE STARTED:	DATE COMPLETED:

CANDLE TYPE ◯ GLASSES ◯JARS ◯OTHER _____

WAX TYPE & BAND	QTY	MELT TEMP	POUR TEMP

ROOM TEMP:	COST:

SUPPLIES USED: _____

ADDITIVES USED: _____

INGREDIENTS	AMOUNT USED / SIZE	NOTES

AMBIENT ROOM TEMP:		NUMBER OF POURS
◯ CONTAINER	◯ MOLD	
COOLING TIME	FINAL PRODUCT	HOT THROW : 1 2 3 4 5
		COLD THROW: 1 2 3 4 5
MELT POOL:	DIFFICULTY	
	◯ EASY ◯MODERATE ◯CHALLENGE	

SCENT
☆☆☆☆☆

BURN LENGTH
☆☆☆☆☆

OVERALL
☆☆☆☆☆

NOTES:
_____
_____
_____
_____
_____
_____

PROJECT:	CREATED FOR:
DATE STARTED:	DATE COMPLETED:

CANDLE TYPE ◯ GLASSES ◯ JARS ◯ OTHER _____

WAX TYPE & BAND	QTY	MELT TEMP	POUR TEMP

ROOM TEMP:	COST:

SUPPLIES USED: _____

ADDITIVES USED: _____

INGREDIENTS	AMOUNT USED / SIZE	NOTES

AMBIENT ROOM TEMP:		NUMBER OF POURS
◯ CONTAINER	◯ MOLD	
COOLING TIME	FINAL PRODUCT	HOT THROW : 1 2 3 4 5
		COLD THROW: 1 2 3 4 5
MELT POOL:	DIFFICULTY	
	◯ EASY ◯ MODERATE ◯ CHALLENGE	

SCENT
☆☆☆☆☆

BURN LENGTH
☆☆☆☆☆

OVERALL
☆☆☆☆☆

NOTES:
_____
_____
_____
_____
_____
_____

PROJECT:	CREATED FOR:
DATE STARTED:	DATE COMPLETED:

CANDLE TYPE ◯ GLASSES ◯ JARS ◯ OTHER _____

WAX TYPE & BAND	QTY	MELT TEMP	POUR TEMP

ROOM TEMP:	COST:

SUPPLIES USED: _____

ADDITIVES USED: _____

INGREDIENTS	AMOUNT USED / SIZE	NOTES

AMBIENT ROOM TEMP:		NUMBER OF POURS
◯ CONTAINER	◯ MOLD	
COOLING TIME	FINAL PRODUCT	HOT THROW : 1 2 3 4 5
		COLD THROW: 1 2 3 4 5
MELT POOL:	DIFFICULTY	
	◯ EASY ◯ MODERATE ◯ CHALLENGE	

SCENT
☆☆☆☆☆

BURN LENGTH
☆☆☆☆☆

OVERALL
☆☆☆☆☆

NOTES: _____
_____
_____
_____
_____
_____

PROJECT:	CREATED FOR:
DATE STARTED:	DATE COMPLETED:

CANDLE TYPE ◯ GLASSES ◯JARS ◯OTHER _____

WAX TYPE & BAND	QTY	MELT TEMP	POUR TEMP

ROOM TEMP:	COST:

SUPPLIES USED: _____

ADDITIVES USED: _____

INGREDIENTS	AMOUNT USED / SIZE	NOTES

AMBIENT ROOM TEMP:		NUMBER OF POURS
◯ CONTAINER	◯ MOLD	
COOLING TIME	FINAL PRODUCT	HOT THROW : 1 2 3 4 5
		COLD THROW: 1 2 3 4 5
MELT POOL:	DIFFICULTY	
	◯ EASY ◯MODERATE ◯CHALLENGE	

SCENT
☆☆☆☆☆

BURN LENGTH
☆☆☆☆☆

OVERALL
☆☆☆☆☆

NOTES: _____
_____
_____
_____
_____
_____

PROJECT:	CREATED FOR:
DATE STARTED:	DATE COMPLETED:

CANDLE TYPE ◯ GLASSES ◯JARS ◯OTHER _____

WAX TYPE & BAND	QTY	MELT TEMP	POUR TEMP

ROOM TEMP:	COST:

SUPPLIES USED: _____

ADDITIVES USED: _____

INGREDIENTS	AMOUNT USED / SIZE	NOTES

AMBIENT ROOM TEMP:		NUMBER OF POURS
◯ CONTAINER	◯ MOLD	
COOLING TIME	FINAL PRODUCT	HOT THROW : 1 2 3 4 5
		COLD THROW: 1 2 3 4 5
MELT POOL:	DIFFICULTY	
	◯ EASY ◯MODERATE ◯CHALLENGE	

SCENT
☆☆☆☆☆

BURN LENGTH
☆☆☆☆☆

OVERALL
☆☆☆☆☆

NOTES: _____
_____
_____
_____
_____
_____

Made in the USA
Monee, IL
05 August 2022